GOD'S DAWN

for every DARKNESS

*Morning-Fresh Glimpses
into His Gracious Heart*

Edward Miller

WATERBROOK
PRESS

GOD'S DAWN FOR EVERY DARKNESS
PUBLISHED BY WATERBROOK PRESS
2375 Telstar Drive, Suite 160
Colorado Springs, Colorado 80920
A division of Random House, Inc.

ISBN 1-57856-139-6

Published in association with the literary agency of Alive Communications, Inc., 7680 Goddard Street, Suite 200; Colorado Springs, Colorado 80920

Library of Congress Cataloging-in-Publication Data
Miller, Edward
    God's dawn for every darkness : morning-fresh glimpses into His gracious heart / by
Edward Miller.— 1st. ed.
        p. cm.
    ISBN 1-57856-139-6
    1. Meditations. I. Title.

BV4832.3 .M55 2001
242—dc21

                                                                00-067315

Printed in the United States of America
2001—First Edition

10 9 8 7 6 5 4 3 2 1

I dedicate this book with profound affection

to my dear wife, Lillian,

who is as perfectly suited by the Lord for my completeness

as Eve was for Adam's.

Contents

When I Am Searching...

When I Am Afraid...

When I Wrestle with Questions…

As I Minister to Others…

Introduction

*T*here is truth that sometimes comes into the childlike heart like a sudden flash from the Lord. In a moment, the Lord is manifested and an insight into His heart and purposes is transformingly implanted. These are glorious experiences of beholding Him and advancing in grace and glory.

There is also truth that is more of a dawning than a flashing; it is the result of a daily pondering by the heart on some word of revelation. By an earnest heart knowledge of God through the faithful study of His word...through worshipful meditation...by faith's application of the principles of the covenant of pure grace to the changing experiences of life...by an intimate fellowship with the living Lord, progressive light is granted to the children of God. This light enables them to "prove [themselves] to be blameless and innocent, children of God above reproach in the midst of a crooked and perverse generation." This insight into God's heart develops in the same way that time ripens precious fruit.

The words in this volume are the gatherings of the light that the Lord has gently showered upon the writer from many different clouds through many years. If the wisdom here is from above, it will be found to be "first pure, then peaceable, gentle, reasonable, full of mercy and good fruits, unwavering, without hypocrisy."

The meditations in this book may be read in any order. All are addressed to those who desire to discover the secrets of God's heart, who long to walk in intimate union with Him. These thoughts are published with the prayer that, if there be any light from heaven in these pages, it might providentially fall upon the path traveled by those who long to walk with God…and that, added together with the light of God from other quarters, it may help illumine the way to Him.

I Discover the Dawn...

1 The Rising Sun, Our Bridegroom

*T*urn your thoughts to the day our Savior died. Think of the supernatural darkness that enveloped the Lord Jesus for the three brightest hours of the day. In your mind's eye, see the sun pulling all of her glories to herself and wrapping herself in sackcloth, in sympathy with the Sun of Righteousness who was spending His last rays on sinful humanity. Hymn writers have personified the sun by describing it as blushing with embarrassment and shame, refusing to shine on so momentous an occasion. Certainly, the sun set when Jesus died!

If the Lord at His death was pictured by the setting sun, would He not be pictured by the rising sun when He arose from the grave on Easter Sunday?

There is a wonderful section of the nineteenth Psalm that describes the glory of the rising sun. Psalm 19:5 describes it as "a bridegroom coming out of his chamber." Isn't that exactly what took place when Jesus rose from the dead? He was the exalted Bridegroom coming out of His chamber. This is what the death and resurrection of the Lord Jesus was all about. He loved us and purchased, from Himself, the right to have a holy union with us.

Whenever you view a sunrise again, think of the glorious resurrection of the Bridegroom, the Lover of your soul!

2 See Him in Scripture, Know Him in Life

No doubt you have sensed an urgency in your heart to be graciously visited by the Lord. I, too, long for Him to unveil Himself to me by life-transforming revelations.

Perhaps your earnest desire to behold the Lord has turned your head in many directions. You wonder, "How will He make Himself known to me? Will I see Him in creation? In my brothers and sisters in Christ? In the changing circumstances of life? By a dream or in a vision?"

And in any of these ways, does the Lord "come and go" in manifesting Himself to us?

Strictly speaking, He cannot "come and go," for He is at all times omnipresent. He may, at special times and for His wise reasons, declare Himself present. He may at other times hide Himself from our knowledge. But it would contradict His nature to actually depart and arrive. Whether or not He grants us a manifestation of Himself, we may comfort our hearts by the truth that He is always there.

Neither does He leave us baffled as to *how* He will manifest Himself to us. O friend in Christ, beyond all doubt, He delights to unveil Himself to the hungry heart, and He will most often do so through the Scriptures.

When the Lord Jesus, after His resurrection, appeared to the two disciples on the road to Emmaus, He was pleased to make Himself known to them by enlightening their minds to the revelation of Himself in the Bible. Although He was then exalted and could have easily dazzled them with a physical vision of His underived glory, He refused to do that. Instead He began with Moses and all the prophets and explained to these two men the things from Scripture concerning Himself. Until He dawned on them in this way, sorrow and unbelief dimmed their eyes. Later, as they reflected on their experience, they confessed that their hearts burned like fire as He manifested Himself from the pages of the Bible.

However, even with this revelation of Him in the Scriptures, even as they walked with Christ, even as their hearts were burning…they were still strangers. Not until later, after they had walked with Him awhile, did they discover Him, when He made Himself known to them in the breaking of the bread.

It is possible to have our hearts burning with excitement because we have seen the Lord in a fresh way in the Scriptures and yet remain strangers to the Lord as far as intimate union is concerned. Our vision of the Lord may be merely academic. Orthodox doctrine is not Christ. It is in fellowship with Jesus that He will be transformingly discovered to our hearts.

That, I think, is why He appears to come and go, arrive and disappear again.

We must see Him in the Scriptures, but we must come to know Him in life. As we enjoy that manifestation of Him in life, He may seem to disappear, but it is only that He might repeat the glorious process all over again. He disappeared from the physical presence of the disciples only to reappear to them in the Upper Room and open their hearts in a fresh way to understand the Scriptures. Appearing and disappearing, progressively opening our eyes to Himself in the Bible—this seems to be His way with His church.

Let us ever look for Him where He has assured us He would be found—in the Bible. Let us pray for each other that Christ would set our hearts on fire as we see Him in the Scriptures and that He would make Himself known to us as we walk in fellowship with Him on all the roads of life.

Rest! Enjoy! Abide! Walk in His light!

3 The Light of Context Illumines God's Heart

*G*od is not in bondage to our principles of interpreting His wonderful Word. He ever meets His children as and where they are in order to bring them to the place He desires them to be.

That is why God can, and often does, reveal Himself through a passage of Scripture apart from its context.

I am not suggesting that the context of a Bible passage should be disregarded; I am only pointing out the fact that God can satisfy the heart before the thirsty child becomes a scholar. When God manifests Himself through any passage of Scripture, the revelation will be consistent with His truth in the balance of Scripture. As you come to understand the context of the verse or verses, the revelation of the Lord Jesus will become more pointed and precious.

Allow me to give two illustrations from my own experience. For many years I have comforted the saints of God with His promise in Isaiah 42, that His presence would support them in the fire and the flood. I understood this promise in terms of the general trials of life. I shared it freely with the prisoner, the tempted, the afflicted, and the shut-in. It was a very precious truth, even detached from its context in Israel's history.

One day the Lord dawned upon my heart the true context of the promise. It was God's promise to preserve His people by His presence even when they passed through the fire and flood of God's chastening. That God would hold the hand of His child when he was called to pass through life's troubles was comfort indeed, but incalculably precious was the wonder that the Lord would not forsake His disobedient child even when passing under the chastening rod. The context brings wonderful light to the one under discipline. Even if God must bring us into confusion and captivity because of our sin, He will continue to hold our hand and pass through the bitter experience with us. Do you see how the context enhances our view of God's heart?

As accurate context enlarges comfort, so it increases conviction. I recall the day I armed myself with a passage of Scripture to offer loving counsel to a brother inclined to gossip. I thought that what God had inspired through James on the subject of the tongue was suited perfectly to his case. As I pored over this passage, preparing my heart to share with him, the first verse of the "tongue chapter," James 3, came home to my spirit with great power and conviction:

> Let not many of you become teachers, my brethren, knowing
> that as such we shall incur a stricter judgment.

The chapter I was applying to gossips was actually written as a warning to guard the tongues of teachers! It is the teacher whose tongue has the power to influence and move a whole body of believers, as a very small rudder can turn a great ship. The true context did not weaken the application to gossips, but it shed a great deal of light on the original intention of God's heart when He first inspired that word. Since that day, the chapter has had a humbling influence on my heart as one privileged to proclaim His truth.

There are, beyond doubt, unlimited applications to every truth of God, but the context wonderfully homes in on the chief intention of the Author.

We can ever praise the Lord that He is not bound to our hermeneutical principles before He can minister to our hearts. Study God's Word to know the Lord; study God's Word in context to know Him better.

4 The Miracle of Morning Devotions

You need not feel embarrassed that you have not the discipline you desire to meet with the Lord in the early morning hours. God intends that we learn our utter helplessness even in those things that bring us the greatest delight and benefit.

There is a precious passage of Scripture that the prophet Isaiah applied to Messiah concerning morning devotions. That this passage refers to our Lord Jesus Christ is beyond doubt, for Isaiah says:

> I gave My back to those who strike Me,
> and My cheeks to those who pluck out the beard;
> I did not cover My face from humiliation and spitting.
>   (Isaiah 50:6)

In this context of describing our Lord Jesus, it is written in the previous verses that His heavenly Father woke Him up every morning so that He might have a disciple's ear and tongue and that He might learn to walk redemptively.

My friend in Christ, if it was true of our Lord Jesus that He was supernaturally enabled to have an early morning intimacy with his Father, how much more do *we* require His grace to awaken us morning by morning and to open our spiritual ears?

Be eager to fellowship with the Lord before the pressures and privileges of the day begin, and be encouraged that such a devotional habit is yours by a miracle of grace.

If the Lord awakens us morning by morning and anoints our ears to hear as disciples, the moments we spend in His presence will be everlastingly precious and fruitful.

As our every attempt of the flesh fails, may the secret of our Lord's devotional life be ours!

May His dew fall daily upon your heart.

5 Christ Shall Dawn on You

*T*here is a tendency in the sensitive child of the New Covenant, in his great desire to please the Lord, to become introspective. You may at times have asked a more mature believer to "brutally examine" your life so that you may discover, and deal with, the slightest thing that is displeasing to the Lord.

I do believe, however, that such a scrutiny by any other but the Lord Himself can be harmful to your walk with Him. We should not only beware of an occupation with self-examination but also be extremely careful in permitting the most trusted confidant to penetrate the secret places of our inner union with God. There is a digging and an introspection that is premature and may actually hinder progress with the Lord.

There is a more excellent way to deal with the mystery of abiding corruption.

When the apostle Paul warned the believers in Ephesians 5 not to participate in the unfruitful works of darkness, he used physical light as an illustration to show them how God would discover and deal with the dark parts of their lives. Just as light exposes things that are hidden in the darkness and the very presence of light expels the darkness, so Christ Himself, who is light, rises upon a believer as the sun rises in the morning. When Christ dawns upon the believer, it is as the dawning of a day before which the darkness of night passes silently away.

The idea of dawning is a wonderful concept. Matthew used the word *dawn* to describe the first Easter morning:

As it began to dawn toward the first day of the week. (28:1)

What the dawn is to the physical world, the revelation of Christ is to the believer. Christ desires to dawn upon every believer.

Awake, sleeper,
And arise from the dead,
And Christ will shine [dawn] on you. (Ephesians 5:14)

Christ will dawn on you! Christ will give you light! In other places in the Scriptures, our dear Lord Jesus is called "the sun of righteousness" and "the day star" and "the bright morning star." God's promise is that the Lord Jesus Christ will dawn on us and, by the glory of His appearing, that our works of darkness will be dissipated. This is God's method of uncovering and removing our sin.

It is by the dawning of Christ and not by a personal introspection that our darkness is discovered. God knows when to dawn upon us. He knows when we are able to bear the sight of our corruption. A vision of our sin, before we are prepared by the revelation of Christ to receive it, would crush us.

There are those who tell us that we must, by searching our hearts, discover our sin before we can turn that sin over to the Lord Jesus. The reality is that we have no more ability to truly discover our sin by introspection than we have to conquer it after it is discovered. We need His revelation to discover our problem; we need His life to solve it. The sight of sin, apart from the vision of the Lord, brings only condemnation. The enemy of our souls has used morbid introspection to bring thousands of God's precious children under condemnation.

We must ever see Christ before we dare behold our sin. Job saw the Lord, then repented of his sin in dust and ashes; Isaiah saw the Lord, high and exalted, then cried out, "Woe is me, I am undone!" It was when Daniel saw the Lord that his comeliness was turned to dust. Peter saw himself as a sinful man only after he beheld the glory of the Lord.

We must see Him first. We must look far away from our own hearts and ever remain focused upon Him. Our Lord Jesus Christ knows when to dawn on us. He knows when we are ready to face our corruption.

"Search me, O God, and know my heart," prayed the psalmist. He did not desire some close brother or sister to examine his heart. It is God who must do the digging. When He searches us, we are assured that what is uncovered will not lead to condemnation.

If we had to search our own hearts, the task would never be finished and we would be forced to live in unbearable discouragement because of what we would daily uncover.

Oh, what a glorious salvation the New Covenant Christian enjoys! God causes Christ to dawn upon His children in the fullness of time. In the glory of the revelation of Jesus, our darkness is dispelled and transformed into day. It is no wonder that we who belong to the Lord are called the children of the day and the sons and daughters of light.

With the dawning of Christ comes the day. The darkness, Paul says (in Ephesians 5:13), is not only displaced by the dawn; it actually becomes the dawn:

> All things become visible when they are exposed by the light, for *everything that becomes visible is light.*

If you desire to walk in an unbroken fellowship with the Lord and you fear the possibility of being deceived by some undetected sin that would threaten that union, I assure you that your fears are groundless. God has shown us the biblical way to deal with the darkness in our lives: The *light* must deal with the darkness. Christ must dawn upon our darkness, and until He does, all our introspection will not expose or expel it.

The Lord is far more concerned than you are that your sweet union with Him be continued. He will certainly reveal to your heart anything that would interfere with that communion. If there is a problem, He will dawn upon you, and by the glory of that revelation, He will transform your heart.

Do not look within! Turn your eyes to Him instead. God is faithful. He will convict you when He knows you are ready to be convicted. Do not trust others to do the work of the Holy Spirit in your life. When Christ dawns upon you, the darkness will flee and your day will be filled with joyful singing.

WHEN I AM DISCOURAGED...

1 God's Paths
Are Never Aimless

*D*o not be discouraged because the Lord has not clearly spelled out for you the wise purposes of His dispensations in your life. "Why doesn't God clearly reveal His will to me?" you may ask. "I feel as if I am running around in circles!" That seems to be a common lament from many pilgrim hearts, and I can identify very well with such frustration.

The apostle Paul informs us that the history of Israel was written for our instruction, and so it is for us on this issue.

Immediately after Israel was redeemed from Egypt, the Lord guided them into confusion. Pharaoh interpreted Israel's direction as "aimless wandering in the wilderness." Was it aimless? Although human wisdom could not detect God's heart, was there not a wise design in their strange path? By omniscience, God anticipated the response His children would have had if they faced the enemy unprepared. He knew that they would become discouraged and desire to turn back.

For that reason He engineered a mysterious by-path by which they could learn to know and trust Him. How necessary was this preparation for His children! Their wandering was far from aimless.

Nothing is aimless that crowds us to Christ and creates a child-like faith in us. The logical path, from earth's low viewpoint, is not always the safest path. Thank God for the by-paths! For Israel, the long, mysterious route was actually the shortcut to God's spiritual objectives.

A second illustration may enforce the same truth. God's chosen people may have wondered why, when there was a war to win and a land to gain, they were commanded to march in circles around Jericho. If you feel you are running in circles, remember that circles are not a bad thing if they are God's circles. We know how great a part in conquering central Palestine those circles were. The day is coming when you will praise the Lord for the very circles that trouble you today.

I am not qualified to shed light on your particular circumstances. I do not know how or for what God is preparing you, but I do feel inclined to remind you of a truth that God's pilgrims in every age must learn and re-learn. The secret of guidance is the guide Himself; the person, not the path. If your eyes remain focused on His glory cloud, your feet will never stray from His path.

Let us, by His grace, be patient.

Not only did God command Israel to march in circles around Jericho, but He also commanded them to renew the covenant of circumcision. By renewing it, God put every soldier who marched around Jericho in the place of an eight-day-old baby. God has called us to walk in helpless dependence upon Him.

It is incidental whether our path be over high mountains, through deep valleys, in a straight line, or in circles on the sand. What is imperative is that we behold Him in childlike faith—the Lord whose will it is. When He grants us the eyes to behold Christ, then we will know in a living way that His ways with us, though confusing, are not aimless.

God rest you!

2 Two Advocates

*I*n 1 John 2:1, our dear Lord Jesus is called the Christian's Advocate who acts in the believer's defense if he sins. The very same word is applied over and over again by the apostle John to the Holy Spirit of God (John 14:16,26; 15:26; 16:7).

This raises an interesting question: Why does the Christian need *two* advocates?

The word we translate "helper" or "comforter" is actually the Greek word *paraclete,* which literally refers to "one who is called alongside to help another." Since both the Lord Jesus and the Holy Spirit are given the title of Advocate, it would be helpful to discover by God's light if their ministry as advocate is identical toward the Christian.

The Lord Jesus stands at the Father's right hand in heaven; the Holy Spirit, as the Life of God, indwells the believer's being. Both are advocates. What is the difference in their ministry as advocate? We would not begin to doubt that our Lord Jesus is all sufficient as our Advocate, defending us perfectly before His holy Father, God. How are we profited by an indwelling Advocate when we have such perfect representation in heaven?

Every advocate must have a client. I believe that if we identify the clients of the two advocates, we will begin to understand why God in His grace has provided two. Beyond all doubt, the Christian is the client of the Advocate who pleads our case in heaven. If any man sins, he has an Advocate with the Father—Jesus Christ the Righteous.

Is the Christian also the client of the Holy Spirit? Is it we who are represented by Him? Is it our cause that He is defending? Whose affairs is the Holy Spirit overseeing? I believe the Holy Spirit is the Advocate of the Lord Jesus Christ. The Christian is not His client. It is the Lord Jesus who is being represented by Him.

Everything the Holy Spirit does is in the name of and for the sake of His client. The Advocate, who lives in my heart and yours, has no self-interest. He lives in us to defend the name and cause of our Lord Jesus. Day by day He safeguards the cause of Jesus. He does not indwell us to guarantee our best interest, but rather the best interest of His client. We have become the inheritance of Christ, and the Holy Spirit is happily employed in safeguarding His purchased property.

Our Advocate (Jesus) is in heaven; the Advocate of Jesus (the Holy Spirit) lives in His people.

Is it not wonderful to realize that the Holy Spirit has full control of all the affairs of His client? He will guard His estate and guarantee His inheritance in the saints.

The Advocate in heaven is there to deal with our sins; the Advocate in our hearts is there to guarantee our holiness.

May you understand more of the Spirit's heart as He fights for the Savior's cause in your life.

3 The Lamb's Book of Life

What is meant by "the Lamb's Book of Life" (Revelation 21:27)? A year ago I could not have offered you a ray of light to help answer that question; now I am excited to share with you the small insight I have been enjoying for many months.

For a number of years I thought of the Lamb's Book of Life as a large registry of names. It was, in my mind, like a huge catalog arranged in alphabetical order, listing the names of those who belonged to the Lord by redemption.

I have lately been convinced, because of the context of the record of the final judgment before the Great White Throne of God, that the book is far more than a registry of names. Those unforgiven sinners who were being judged by God were judged "out of the books." Clearly, they are record books. God has kept records on every individual who has ever lived, and by those records—based on the light of revelation they have received—they will all be justly judged. It was in the context of the record books that we read, "Another book was opened, which was the book of life." In Revelation that book is called "the Lamb's Book of Life."

Since the other books are record books, is it not possible that this, too, is a record book? The Lamb's book of life is the record of the Lamb's life! Oh, what a sterling record that must be! It contains the perfect record of the impeccable Savior. For thirty-three and one half years He lived on the Earth and did always those things that pleased the Father. He never once sinned in thought, word, deed, or the profound intentions of the heart. Satan found nothing in Him that could incline Him to sin. The Lamb's Book of Life is the perfect record of the Lord Jesus as He lived on the Earth.

What must it mean to have my name written in that book? It must be that His perfect record is imputed to me. Under *my* name are listed *His* perfections. What a glorious thought to contemplate! Jesus became sin for me, and I have become the righteousness of God in Him. We traded record books! He took mine to the cross and grave; I will take His to heaven.

How can there be any condemnation for those whose names are written in the Lamb's Book of Life? When God looks for our names, He will find them in the book that belongs to Jesus. The Lamb's perfect record will be credited to us.

How much more is the Lamb's Book of Life than a registry of names? It is the imputed record of the Holy Son of God to every forgiven sinner.

No doubt there is more to it than I have shared, but this is the light that has melted my thankful heart for many months.

If I could digest the full meaning of it, I would probably better understand why the Lord Jesus told us to rejoice more in the fact that our names are written in heaven then in the fact that He has given us authority over demons.

4　The Ministry of Snow

I know it's easy to become discouraged when we judge things by their outward appearance, especially as regards the results of our ministry.

Visible response is not always reliable. In the parable Jesus told of the sower, the seed that fell on rocky soil "received the word with joy." One could easily judge this response as favorable, yet we read that it had no firm root and that, under the heat of temptation, it withered away. Outward responses can be deceptive.

Two times the apostle Paul requested prayer from his brothers and sisters in Christ using the expression "as I ought to speak." In his epistle to the Ephesian Christians he requested prayer that he might "make known with boldness the mystery of the gospel…as I ought to speak" (6:19-20, ASV). To the Colossian Christians he sought for intercession for his ministry of the Word, that he might "make it clear in the way I ought to speak" (4:4).

This also is the right prayer for your ministry and mine: that we would speak both boldly and clearly, as we ought to speak. And after praying it, we must prayerfully leave the results with Him. The seed has been scattered on the soils of hearts. The Lord is still accomplishing the real work.

Deep down in your spirit, you must be assured that the government of your ministry rests squarely on His shoulders. Surely the Lord speaks to hearts through our ministries.

It is not, after all, the word which proceeds out of *our* mouths that is promised success; instead the Lord's promise reads, "*My* word...which goes forth from *My* mouth...will not return to Me empty" (Isaiah 55:11).

The metaphors that Isaiah uses to deliver this promise are full of comfort:

> As the *rain* and the *snow* come down from heaven,
> And do not return there without watering the earth
> And making it bear and sprout...
> So will My word be which goes forth from My mouth.

We, as His instruments, are not only likened to rain, but also to the snow. Snow has a ministry. The winter is as important to the spring as the spring is to the harvest.

I realize that it's very pleasant to be used by the Lord as rain—or, as Moses says, to have our speech "distill as the dew, as the droplets on the fresh grass and as the showers on the herb" (Deuteronomy 32:2). However, our hearts naturally recoil when He desires to use us as the snow. When the delivery of His message seems cold, when the response to it appears chilly, when the whole atmosphere seems to be filled with a frosty unfriendliness—then our spirits are heavy and we sense that our ministry has failed.

My friend in Christ, let us trust God and believe that our winter ministry is never wasted. Rejoice! For whether it is rain or snow, it is all God's work and will finally succeed in the matter to which God sent it. It is God's business to use us as rain or snow, according to His good pleasure. It is our business to be available to minister in faith.

Do not let the north wind rob you of your rest.

5 Running the Race

*A*lthough, it is true that believers in the Lord Jesus are never to be victims of the past and live under condemnation, yet there is a blessed ministry in looking back. If the backward look encourages the upward look, it can be healthy indeed. The past often encourages present faith. When the apostle Paul encouraged the Philippian believers to forget the things that were behind so that they might concentrate on the prize before them, I do not believe he was ruling out every memory of redemptive history.

In the context of the portion of the letter that counsels them to forget, Paul was describing the Christian life as a footrace. Looking back would be a great hindrance to the spiritual runner. We must forget all those things that, if remembered, would hinder the race. There is a way, however, to look back at the past that would not hinder the race. If we look back at past defeats in our lives, for example, and realize that they are under the precious blood of Jesus, then we will not be running under condemnation.

There is also a way to remember past victories that will not enable us to run better. We must realize that the grace of yesterday will not support us in the present moment. We need to continually keep our eyes on the Lord Jesus, that He might continually pluck our feet out of the net. We must always check our looking back by the question "Does this enable me to run the race better, or does it hinder my running?"

Thank God, there is a looking back that is healthy and actually helps us as Christian athletes. When David was about to face the giant Goliath, he recalled his personal redemptive history, and drew great encouragement from it. There was a time in his life when a lion seized a lamb from his flock, and the Lord enabled David to kill the lion and rescue the little lamb. There was another time that he confronted a bear, and when the bear sought to maul him, the power of the Lord came upon him and enabled him to bring the bear down by his beard. David remembered those great victories in his past, and from them he found the courage to face Goliath by the name and life of the Lord. His past enabled him to run better in the present.

If what God has done for us in the past quickens our faith to trust Him in a fresh way, then the memory has not at all hindered the race. Remembering the faithfulness of God, and what He has already done for us, may be exactly what is needed to turn our eyes toward Him in the present moment.

In Isaiah 43:18-19, God says:

Do not call to mind the former things,
Or ponder things of the past. Behold, I will do
    something new.

He also says, in 46:9:

Remember the former things long past,
For I am God, and there is no other;
I am God, and there is no one like Me.

Press on, friend. There is an upward call of God in Christ Jesus, and we have not yet arrived. We are in the final lap and the ribbon is in view. By all means, let us forget everything behind us that would in any way hinder the race, but let us recall with humble gratitude those countless times when His grace was sufficient for us and His fellowship was a present help in trouble. Those memories call us to faith and quicken our pace.

6 A Prophet's Reward

*P*erhaps you have thought with disappointment that you will have very few crowns to cast at the deserving feet of the dear Lord Jesus in the day of glory for the church, as represented by the twenty-four elders in Revelation 4:10. No lover of Jesus would want to miss the joy of that anointing. There is little doubt that some will have more honor to bestow upon Jesus than others will have, but that difference is not due to the number of talents entrusted to each Christian. Faithfulness, not success, is the great issue by which rewards will be determined.

The concept of casting crowns at the feet of Jesus may only be a powerful word picture of our worship and His exaltation, but since the reality is always greater than the picture, if it is not literal, then it will be infinitely more wonderful. Every Christian will be amazed and humbled by the Lord's merciful heart in distributing rewards.

Jesus said, "He who receives a prophet in the name of a prophet shall receive a prophet's reward; and he who receives a righteous man in the name of a righteous man shall receive a righteous man's reward. And whoever in the name of a disciple gives to one of these little ones even a cup of cold water to drink, truly I say to you, he shall not lose his reward" (Matthew 10:41-42).

Can you picture the widow of Zarephath who lived in the days of the prophet Elijah, or the Shunamite woman and her husband who lived in the days of Elisha the prophet, when God bestows upon them the prophet's reward?

Because each person ministered unto God's prophet, each had a part in the prophet's ministry. God has recorded the influence each had in the life of His servant, and that influence united each one to the prophet's ministry. The widow of Zarephath will be rewarded for the contest with Baal on Mount Carmel; the Shunamite couple will be rewarded for the healing of Naaman the leper. They received the prophet, and so they share in the prophet's reward.

The writer of Hebrews reminds us:

> God is not unjust so as to forget your work and the love which
> you have shown toward His name, in having ministered and in
> still ministering to the saints.

God keeps perfect track of those who watch the baggage as well as those who fight on the front lines. Your service may be quiet and behind the scenes here, but in the day of His coronation you will be weighted down with glory to pour upon Him. Be faithful and keep handing out those refreshing cups of water in His name, and you will not lack crowns to cast at His lovely feet!

7 Sitting Down with Jesus

*H*ow wonderful it is to know that our Lord Jesus has already accomplished everything that ever needs to be done for our redemption for the past, for the present moment, and for all the long ages of eternity. The keynote of finality should be ever ringing in our hearts!

Four times in the wonderful book of Hebrews, the Holy Spirit said of our Lord Jesus that He sat down. Hebrews 10:11-13 contrasts the standing priests, whose work was never finished, to the sitting Lord Jesus, whose amazing work was once done and forever completed. He could sit down at the right hand of the throne of the Majesty in the heavens because His work was finished.

As I pondered this glorious picture of our Lord Jesus, sitting down because His redemptive work was finished, I began to meditate on Paul's words in Ephesians 2:4-6:

> But God, being rich in mercy, because of His great love with which He loved us, even when we were dead in our transgressions, made us alive together with Christ (by grace you have been saved), and raised us up with Him, and seated us with Him in the heavenly places in Christ Jesus.

My first thought was, "How gloriously simple this is! Christ has finished redemption's work! He is seated in the heavens. All I need to do to enjoy His redemption is to sit down with Him by faith. By a child's trust I may be completely satisfied with His completed work." I reasoned, "That is my part. I must sit down with Jesus!"

But, my friend, how quickly the Holy Spirit delivered my heart from a covenant of works. I do not need to sit down with Jesus. The truth is even more wonderful. I must believe that I am already sitting down in Him. There is nothing I have to do to identify with my seated Savior.

I am so thankful that the Lord flashed that reality in my heart, or I would have been struggling with trying to sit down with Jesus and then wondering why it was such a bondage to do such a simple thing.

Blessed be our Lord! He has finished the work! He sat down at the right hand of His Holy Father, God. When He sat down, I sat down. It is a fact that when He sat down, the whole church sat down. All who would ever be in union with Jesus were seated with Him in heavenly places. It is a gospel fact.

8 The Elder Shall Serve the Younger

*I*f you have ever grieved over the abiding corruption of the heart, you are not the first believer in the Lord to do so. How we all long to be forever rid of the tendency to dishonor the Lord! How we will rejoice when the great Babylon of the flesh is finally thrown down and the bride has made herself ready to be presented to her Groom.

As a brother in grace, I remind you that there is a principle in that ancient promise to Isaac and Rebekah of the elder serving the younger, and that truth shall stand.

Measured in time, your natural birth came years before your spiritual birth. Although your natural birth is older, it will one day, by the good grace of God, bow down to the younger. The flesh is the firstborn, but the promise of lordship falls to the younger—the spiritual.

In our eager desire to see the spirit reign over the flesh, we must not fall into the pitfalls that ensnared our father, Jacob. God must subdue the firstborn; all of our attempts to bring our flesh under submission will backfire.

It is frustrating to see the birthright and the blessing in the possession of the flesh, but we must wait for the Lord to fulfill His own promise. Jacob erred greatly and reaped painful consequences by attempting to wrest God's benediction from the mighty grip of the firstborn.

Yes, there is a struggle between the flesh and the spirit; yes, it sometimes appears that the elder nature is winning and that the younger nature will never take root and thrive; but we stand on the unchanging rock of the grace of God. In due time, the elder will become the slave of the younger.

We struggle. We pray. We strive. We rest. We war. We wait. How those brother natures contend within the confines of the human heart! The day will surely come when the child of promise within us will gain the ascendancy over our natural tendencies. Until that day, we will cling to the promise that the birthright and the blessing will finally belong to the child of God's pleasure.

Christ has redeemed us from the penalty of sin by His own precious blood; such an awesome price also demands redemption from the dominion of sin.

Rejoice! The days of the elder nature are numbered.

9 The Willing Spirit

*M*ay the Lord revive your drooping spirit by a revelation of Himself as *the One who lifts up your head.*

We may have many reasons to be humbled before the Lord, but we have not a single reason to ever remain discouraged before Him. We may describe ourselves as "smoking flax" and a "bruised reed," but is that reason to be discouraged? Has He not promised to be tender with the dying spark and the wounded reed? When He mildly rebuked the disciples for their feeble faith, didn't His question, "Why did you doubt?" contain the implication that there was no reason to doubt or be discouraged?

You may in a slight way identify with Peter, but do not let a harsh inventory of the reality of your spiritual life number you with those in the camp of Judas.

Our Lord Jesus made the difference between Peter's denial and Judas's betrayal. Peter had a willing spirit, although his flesh was weak; Judas did not have a willing spirit. Peter failed because he trusted his own strength instead of the Lord, but in his spirit he always desired to honor the Lord.

A spark is the same in kind as the flame. You may not have the faith you desire in degree, but you have it in kind. Struggling faith is genuine faith. Struggling faith has the desire to believe; unbelief does not have the desire to believe. God regards feeble faith as faith nevertheless, although it may be weak and vacillating.

Dear friend in Christ, you are not an unbeliever. God places great value on the willing spirit. Your weakness does not disqualify you from the free mercy of the Lord.

If you must, go out with Peter and weep bitterly, but then, with him, return, confess your love to the Lord, and grow in grace and the knowledge of Christ.

There is never any cause for any Christian at any time in any condition to remain discouraged. You are in Christ Jesus! Ask your soul honestly why it is cast down. I pray you will not be as Rachel and refuse the comfort I offer in the name of the Lord. Allow Him to lift up your head!

10 The Humped-Over Woman

*H*ave you sighed over the fact that you seem at times to be incurably attracted to the things of this world, even though you know them to be vain and vexatious? This lament finds a similar chord in my heart. I can also relate to the frustration of never being rid of the abiding corruption in the heart. I, too, desire to live a consistently holy life before the Lord.

As I meditated upon these two thorns that commonly plague the souls of God's children, I thought about the precious record Luke gives of the poor woman who was bent double for eighteen long years. I thought, "Here is a woman whose deformed body perfectly illustrates the spiritual realities that plague the earnest Christian."

Her spine was so deformed that the woman could do nothing but look at the earth. She was locked into a focus on this world. The psalmist described a day in which his soul had sunk down to the dust and his body was cleaving to the earth. Oh, how I hate it when I cleave to the earth. This dear child of Abraham, as she was called, was certainly not able to look up. Just so, Luke also describes her as not being able to straighten up. She could not walk upright. That expression *walking upright* is well known in the Holy Scriptures. It describes the godly; they who fear God walk uprightly.

Now I realize that it is only her physical body that illustrates these principles. I would not dare read ill into the motives of her heart or suggest that she was looking away from the Lord to gaze upon this earth. She may well have been living a holy life, though in the body she could not walk upright. I only use her affliction as an illustration of those two burdens that lie daily on the shoulders of the most earnest Christian: She was looking at the earth, and she could not walk upright.

I am revived in my spirit when I see how graciously the Lord dealt with her. I can picture this woman who had been humped over for eighteen years as she shuffled her way from her seat in the synagogue to stand in her pitiful condition before the Savior at His invitation. It was then she heard His liberating words:

Woman, you are freed from your sickness.

What a glorious word indeed! After eighteen years He declared her free, but it was not until He laid His hands upon her that what was objectively true became a subjective reality to her. In that glorious moment she was made erect and she began to praise and glorify God.

Even now, as I write these words and meditate upon these things, my heart is filled with song and hope for the promise of His word and touch. Is it possible that I can look away from this earth, though Satan desires to hold my focus on this vanity? Can I really be set free from all of my anxieties and frettings? By His word and touch, I can. Is it possible that I can walk upright before God and man in spite of the natural tendencies of my natural heart? By His miracle I can. His word declares it; His touch guarantees it.

I am, by faith, as free from anxiety and sin as this woman was when Jesus turned her eyes away from this world to look full in His beautiful face. He enabled her to walk erect, without a period of convalescence, even though her spine was set in its ways. We need not as Christians be humped over and unable to look up or walk upright.

Our Lord Jesus desires that we draw near to Him that He might touch us afresh.

It feels so good to stand up straight and look at Him.

Let us continually glorify the Lord.

WHEN I FEEL OVERWHELMED...

1 Beyond Natural Limits

D on't be surprised or caught unprepared if the Lord Jesus allows you, as He permitted the apostle Paul, to be "burdened excessively, beyond our strength...in order that we should not trust in ourselves, but in God who raises the dead" (2 Corinthians 1:8-9). Perhaps there have been times when you told yourself, in trusting patience, "God will not give me more than I can bear!" I hope your understanding of that concept includes the fuller truth, "He will not give me more than I can bear when I am trusting Jesus!" Faith can always bear more than flesh can bear.

It is often God's high purpose to push us beyond the thresholds of human endurance so we may learn the wonder of living by His life. It is when we are beyond the limits of natural ability that we enjoy resurrection. It is when our courage is exhausted, our strength is spent, our resources are depleted, and our situation is hopeless that we can depend upon the One who raises the dead.

When God drove the apostle Paul beyond what he could bear, so that Paul confessed that he despaired even of life, he was able to bear his test, by the grace of God, to the honor and reputation of God.

In the same way, God will enable you to bear, by grace, the very severe test He has allowed in your life. You must trust Him for the grace to look away from every threshold, every limit, that lies within you naturally and to look to Him alone who is your Sufficiency.

In all cases, Proverbs 28:26 holds true: "He who trusts his own heart is a fool." That is especially the case when we try to depend upon our own courage. We are naturally chicken-hearted, and it takes very little to spend our own adequacy. We quickly come to the end of our natural courage. But whether it is natural courage or natural wisdom or natural strength or natural righteousness, we must never prove ourselves fools by trusting ourselves.

The Lord is far more concerned that we know Him in His all-sufficient fullness than that we become sufficient in ourselves in the day of trouble. He may indeed drive you beyond yourself that you may experience Him.

In that situation, perhaps you have groaned, but I hope that, to His glory, you have not grumbled. Though you feel much, I hope you are not fretting or fainting. Instead may you know the Lord and the sweet fellowship He shares with those who are "burdened excessively...beyond strength." He will never allow more than faith can bear.

Rest!

2 God Bears Us Through Life

*T*he Lord will never stop bearing our burdens. He does better than that. In fact, He carries us!

A chief difference between the idolater and the child of the true and living God, the prophet reminds us in Isaiah 46, is that the idolater is cumbered with the weight of his god, while the Lord is the One who carries His people.

Isaiah reminds us that the Lord has borne us from the moment we were born, and He will continue to carry us even to our old age and graying years. Artists often picture parents and grandparents holding their small children in their arms, but Isaiah paints a picture for our spirits that is even more wonderful to conceive. The Lord holds and caresses an old saint the same way He would cuddle a child. I picture grandmothers and grandfathers in His arms. Isaiah piles comfort on comfort in his word picture. The Lord not only bears burdens, He bears all burdens. He not only bears all burdens, He bears all burdens at all times. He not only always carries all burdens, He carries all those who are burdened. From the womb to the graying years, the Lord will never set His child down.

What a precious hope for those of us whose years are swiftly drawing to a close. As the lesser lights grow dim, the burdens increase, and our feeble frames grow weary, it is comforting to know that the Lord will carry us all the way to heaven.

If you're blessed by the fact that the Lord carries your burdens, may these thoughts increase your joy a thousandfold.

3 His Rest Is Ours

*T*he Lord invites His children to enter into His rest. Over and over again the writer of Hebrews calls our attention to the fact that God Himself is enjoying rest. God is completely free from anxiety and care about all things. After all, He is the One who wields absolute control over everything. It is impossible for God to fret or worry. He is a God who is always at peace, and He is tranquil about every event in the universe.

It would be a wonderful thing if God promised only to give the believer something called rest, a gift of peace that He would bestow upon His own when they are in crisis or facing ominous uncertainty. Even if He granted only that gift in the response to childlike faith, it would be a very precious blessing.

However, the rest the Lord offers to His believing children is something more; it is the very rest *He* enjoys. It is not only His rest in the sense that He is the Author and Source of the rest, but it is His because He is experiencing it. God is perfectly at rest. He is perfectly free from those things that rattle us and test our faith. How separated from fear and anxiety do you suppose the Lord is from the events that hasten us to prayer?

God is inviting us to draw near to Him and discover the rest He is enjoying. He desires that we be as free from a troubled spirit as He is free. As we have trusted Him for imputed righteousness, He desires that we trust Him for imputed rest.

We have no doubt begun to learn that there are times in our lives when He will give us strength in answer to our prayer, but it is His greater desire to reveal *Himself* as our Strength. He will certainly send help to His people, but He would rather we discover that He Himself is our Help. He will give wisdom to those who ask, but better far is the realization that He is made to us Wisdom.

I know He will give you rest when you petition Him, but He may be inviting you to enter into His rest that you might share His peace. There are a million light-years between the rest God enjoys and the rest He grants in answer to believing prayer. He invites us to both. We may receive rest. We may enter into His rest.

Rest belongs to His children. Some, by His mercy, have learned to receive rest as a gift of grace from His hand; others (may God increase their number) have drawn close to the Lord Himself by faith and are sharing the rest that He enjoys by reason of His sovereignty.

The more we enter into His rest and abide there, the less we will need a rest of our own. It is pleasing to the Lord when by faith we see ourselves in Christ Jesus sharing all that belongs to Him.

May God grace us to enter into His rest.

4 Committing Our Children to the Lord

*A*ugustine said of his mother, Monica, that she labored more over his spiritual birth than when she brought him physically into this world. There is a spiritual travail that Christian parents endure for their children. The burden you may have concerning your own child and the struggle you may experience in your heart to yield your child over to the Lord are very common in the lives of believing parents. Your burden is compounded if your beautiful daughter or son will soon be outside the protection of your sanctifying influence. We may receive encouragement and instruction from the faith of Moses' parents.

When they found that they could no longer hide Moses under their protection, by faith they carefully laid him in an ark that they had patterned after Noah's ark and placed him in the river of death. The Nile River seemed the most unlikely place believing parents would yield their sons to the Lord, yet that is exactly what Moses' parents did.

The ark, as a picture of spiritual truth, foreshadowed the Savior. The Nile River was certainly the place of death. How many thousands of Hebrew babies were drowned in the Nile we are not told, but we know it was very many. By that wonderful act of faith, Moses' parents surrendered their son into the faithful hands of God for His protection and for His everlasting purposes.

We know the glorious ending of the story. Moses was not only safe in the ark of God upon the river of death, but it was by that very surrender that God raised Moses up to be a mighty man of God.

We can do no less with our own children. By faith we must release them to the Lord. I know this seems very frightening to the flesh—to place them in that dangerous river—yet it is by this surrender that our faith as parents is tested. Our children are safe in the ark of Christ. When we deliver them to the world, we are, in reality, placing them in the hands of the Lord. Our children are far safer in the world in the hands of the Lord than they would be in the safety of our home and hands.

Surrendering our children to the Lord is the safest thing we can ever do for them. What seems like a death for us will become a resurrection for our children.

May the Lord grace you to humbly place your Moses in the ark of Christ and then yield him unto the Lord. The Nile has no power over our children, except to deliver them safely over to the perfect will of God.

There will be no regrets.

5 Grace All the Way

I know by His light, and by my own experience with Him, how trying it is to attempt to balance our responsibilities toward God with His grace toward us. The answer to the problem is actually as simple as it seems to be complicated. His part is always pure grace; our part is ever to respond positively to Him by the grace He provides. If we would only allow God to do His part, how dynamic our Christian life would be!

In Galatians 3, Paul referred to the beginning and the end of the Christian experience. "How did you begin?" he asks. "Did you receive the Spirit by the works of the Law, or by hearing with faith? Are you so foolish? Having begun by the Spirit, are you now being perfected by the flesh?"

There is no controversy as to how we began our union with the Lord. It was by God's pure grace that we began. We were saved by grace through faith. Our salvation came to us as God's free gift from heaven. There was not a drop of human contribution in the way we began. He offered Himself to us and He enabled us to receive Him. By pure grace we were born again. That is how we began.

The apostle also has a great deal to say about the way our salvation will be consummated. A very glorious day lies before us when our mortal being shall put on immortality; the body of our humble state will be conformed to the body of His glory. Whether we are alive when our change comes, or whether we are long at rest with those who have died in Jesus when the Lord descends from heaven with a shout, by the glory and power of God there will be a resurrection and a rapture that can be attributed only to His power and grace. Who would dare suggest that any man's works would have the smallest part in the consummation of salvation? The final day will be as the first day. It will be a day of grace.

Why is it that we struggle so in the middle? If we begin our experience with the Lord by the pure grace of God without any assistance by our works...if we shall finally be raised up from these corruptible bodies into the presence of the Lord to live and worship Him forever by the unassisted grace of God...then why do we vainly think He needs our help to sanctify us in the little moment we call life?

We could do nothing to commence our spiritual lives beyond receiving Him; we will be able to do nothing to assist Him in restoring us from dust and decay to share in His glory. Why do we imagine we must continue differently than we first began and will finally end? Why can't we learn to walk in Him as we received Him, and as He will finally receive us one day? It cannot be grace at the beginning and at the end and works in the middle. It must be pure grace all the way. It is a sad commentary on our fallen nature that we would begin by grace and end by grace and never realize that it must be God's grace from beginning to end.

Our part in our union with Him is to allow Him to do His part. He is ever giving us His Son. Our entire Christian lives must be a series of receivings. Every time the Holy Spirit proposes the Lord Jesus to our hearts, we are to humbly receive Him by faith. It is by receiving the Lord Jesus in all the infinite wonder of His person that we learn to live by pure grace. All of the changes that we so desire to take place in our lives will be realized as the fruit of our union with Him by grace.

Grace is the bud; glory is the bloom. Here we move from

strength to strength, from faith to faith, from grace to grace, and from glory to glory. It begins with Jesus, it ends with Jesus, and it is Jesus in between.

"For from Him and through Him and to Him are all things. To Him be the glory forever. Amen."

WHEN I AM SEARCHING...

1 We Pray for Light; God Sends Darkness

Recently my son-in-law shared a paradox from the life of Moses with me that I had not before observed in my personal study. Moses longed to know the Lord intimately, and he prayed, "I pray Thee, show me Thy glory!" I cannot imagine a more complete prayer than the prayer to see the glory of God.

God's answer to that prayer has instructed hungry Christians through the centuries. Moses was commanded to stand on a great rock. Before God passed by the rock, He placed Moses in the cleft, then covered the opening with His hand. In that way Moses would be sheltered from the consuming glory of the Lord and be enabled from the safety of the rock to behold God's goodness passing by.

Moses had to be hidden in the cleft of a rock and be sheltered by God's hand, and he was permitted to view only the back of God and not His face—these facts illustrate how holy God is and how feeble man's capacity is to behold Him in full view.

The paradox that struck me so profoundly in this passage was that God revealed His glory through darkness. Moses prayed for light; he prayed to see the glory of God. When the Lord answered that prayer, He actually brought much darkness into Moses' life. It must have been dark in the cave already, but when God's great hand covered the entrance of the cleft, how dark it must have become!

From a recent meditation on the same passage, I knew that I had to abide in Christ and His finished work—just as Moses had to abide in the cleft of the rock—if I really desire to see the glory of God. Now I am beginning to understand how God shows His glory. When I pray for light, He often sends darkness. I seek earnestly to be enlightened through His Word, to know Him better, and I find myself in a narrow place, and darkness sweeps like a great shadow over my soul.

It was God's hand that brought darkness into Moses' life, and I have no doubt it is His hand that brings darkness to me. We pray for light, God sends darkness, and shortly afterward we experience His wonderful goodness pass by. Our prayer is answered. We have seen the glory of the Lord. The light we sought came in the form of darkness…and by it, we behold His glory. Oh, how wonderful are His ways!

Thinking on these things has given me a fresh perspective on darkness. Rather than thinking that my prayer to see His glory was not immediately honored, I now suspect the opposite is true. I now view darkness as the precursor to His goodness. It is delightful to see the glory of God from the security of our union with Jesus.

Only His grace can teach us such realities!

2 His Father's Everything

*B*elievers in the Lord, because of their intimate relationship to Jesus, have certain claims on Him that those who are strangers to Him cannot enjoy. For example, because we belong to Him by redemption, we are guaranteed that the Lord will hear and answer our prayers. No doubt the Lord *hears* the prayers of the unbeliever too, but they have no promise or right to claim His answers. Many are the prerogatives we enjoy as the children of God. The Lord Jesus said, "For whoever does the will of God, he is My brother and sister and mother."

However, some have gone beyond the bounds of privilege and have abused the truth by taking advantage of their union with Jesus. Some imagine themselves exempt from the common troubles of life because they have a relationship with Jesus. Not a few have supposed that their intimate fellowship with God through the Lord Jesus has lifted them above suffering and affliction and disease. They have reasoned that God's covering would protect them from the common trials of life and from mistreatment by sinners.

There is a passage in the Scriptures that can safeguard us with the proper balance of truth in understanding how we can expect God to act toward us because of our union with Jesus. I am referring to Luke's record of Jesus' behavior toward His mother and stepfather when He was twelve years old.

As the mother of Jesus, Mary had certain expectations of how Jesus should behave toward her. There was a profound measure of respect and common courtesy that she expected from Him as child to parent.

Our Lord Jesus remained in Jerusalem after the Passover festivities without seeking His parent's permission or without informing anyone of His intentions. When the parents finally discovered that the twelve-year-old Jesus was not in the family caravan, they became very worried. In fact, as parents they were quite offended by His behavior, as Mary's question to Jesus (in Luke 2:48) seemed to indicate: "Son, why have You treated us in this way? Behold, Your father and I have been anxiously looking for You."

In the answer our Lord Jesus gave to His concerned parents, we see revealed the very heart of God. And from that revelation we learn what we can expect from Him because of our special union with Him. Jesus said, "Did you not know that I had to be in My Father's house?"

Some translations say, "about My Father's business." Actually, in the language Jesus spoke, He did not use the word that we translate as "business" or "affairs" or "house." In the Greek language, Jesus said only, "Did you not know that I had to be about my Father's."

The translators added the word *house* or *business* or *interests* in order to clarify what Jesus really meant. Jesus was occupied with His Father's...EVERYTHING! He had to be about His Father's pleasure, purpose, business, work, affairs, interests, house—everything that was His Father's. Jesus was occupied with the Father's will.

It's as if Jesus had said, "I have a wonderful relationship with you, Mother; I also have a wonderful relationship with My holy Father, God! My relationship with My Father in heaven is higher than My relationship with you. You must expect nothing from my relationship with you that would not be in accordance with My relationship with My holy Father, God. My relationship with you is in terms of My relationship with Him. Your wishes must always serve His will!"

This is the truth that Mary pondered in her heart. We must ponder it as well. When it appears that He has not treated us properly, it is good to remember that what He allows in our lives is perfectly consistent with the Father's good pleasure.

All of Christ's dealings with us are in terms of His union with His Father. The only things we can expect because of our relationship with Him are those things that promote the Father's glory.

Let us enjoy our blessed union with Christ. May He grace us, because of His higher union with the Father, to never question His dealings with us.

3   His Lovingkindness Is Everlasting

We are not always aware of the Lord's providential dealings in our lives. He delivers us daily, and we do not realize it.

We are much like those in Jesus' day who passed by the lily without considering how it grew and passed by the bird without considering how perfectly it was cared for by God. We miss so much by not being alert to God's hand all around us. It is good to pause now and then and look back over our lives, with an eye on the Lord, and reflect on how faithful He has been.

Let me call your attention to Psalm 136. It begins and ends with thanksgiving, and throughout, this phrase is repeated twenty-six times: "The lovingkindness of the Lord is everlasting."

When I read through the entire psalm and deleted that refrain, I was left with only a rather cold historical record. I am so thankful that between every line of Israel's history the Holy Spirit has written this truth: "The lovingkindness of the Lord is everlasting."

I must be more awake to read between the lines of my own history. Already I can see that His lovingkindness laces the events of my life as surely as it did the history of the messianic nation. Perhaps it will take the light of eternity to fully illumine how His love undergirds the whole of my life, but I am challenged to be more God-centered and to read His heart between the lines. Life is too short to pass through it oblivious to the One who governs behind the scene.

Day by day since I have paused to consider Him, I have grown in my awareness of His love and presence, and my vision of Him is increasing. Let me challenge you to see Him in all.

As I once read through Psalm 136 deleting the repeated expression, so I reread it and this time deleted the history. Again and again, twenty-six times, I read the wonderful words, "The lovingkindness of the Lord is everlasting." It struck me that, although I sometimes struggle to see the Lord between the lines of my personal history, a day is soon coming when only that which has been written between the lines will endure. Only His love is everlasting; my history is swiftly passing away and will soon come to an end.

It's no wonder that this psalm begins and ends with a thank-you.

4 The Lamb Shall Shepherd Us

Our Lord is revealed in Scripture as the Good Shepherd who lays down His life for the sheep, as the Great Shepherd who presently intercedes for us at the right hand of God, and as the Chief Shepherd and Bishop of our souls who shall soon return to receive us unto Himself. All these revelations of Christ as shepherd deserve our meditation; none is a higher revelation than the other.

And may I point to another revelation of Christ as shepherd that has recently brought great waves of consolation to my spirit. It is the description of Jesus in Revelation 7:17:

> For the Lamb in the center of the throne will be their shepherd,
> and will guide them to springs of the water of life; and God will
> wipe every tear from their eyes.

The Lamb will be their shepherd. How tender are those words! What a glorious mixing of metaphors! The Lamb is the Shepherd. The fact that He is pictured as the Lamb and that He is reigning from the center of the throne seems to summarize God's great redemptive heart. His lordship and atonement are indissolubly united. He reigns in eternity as the Lamb. There He will shepherd His people to springs of living water.

This same verse also pictures Him as God, wiping all tears from every eye. Could there be a higher revelation of God as the Shepherd than this? What could possible be more tender than a lamb being the shepherd? What is more tender than almighty God's wiping away human tears?

O friend, such a shepherd is ours! The Lamb is my Shepherd, I shall not want. The Lamb makes me lie down in green pastures; the Lamb leads me beside quiet waters; the Lamb restores my soul; the Lamb guides me in the paths of righteousness for His name's sake. Even though I walk through the valley of the shadow of death, I fear no evil for the Lamb is with me; the rod of the Lamb and the staff of the Lamb, they comfort me. The Lamb prepares a table before me in the presence of my enemies; the Lamb has anointed my head with oil; my cup overflows. Surely goodness and lovingkindness will follow me all the days of my life, and I will dwell in the house of the Lamb forever.

The Lamb will shepherd them. I pray that this eternal truth might find a present reality in your heart as you grow in your union with your Shepherd.

There are springs of water, even now, into which He desires to tenderly lead us; there are tears in our eyes, even in time, which none but God can wipe away.

May this tender side of our Shepherd greatly minister to your heart as He feeds you from the center of His throne.

5 His Arms Always Stretched Out

*D*oes the Lord ever get tired of blessing us?

No, He never does. He has given us His Son, and with Him He freely gives us all things. He is a God who loves to bless His people.

Perhaps God intended to convey His everlasting disposition to bless by describing for us (in Luke 24:50-51) the physical posture of our Lord Jesus as He ascended into heaven. Luke writes:

> And He led them out as far as Bethany, and He lifted up His hands and blessed them.
>
> While He was blessing them, He parted from them.

The Lord Jesus ascended with His arms stretched out in priestly benediction.

As far as the Bible record goes, He never put down His hands. Though I am sure He eventually put His arms down to His sides, by not mentioning it, the Bible illustrates the eternity of the Lord Jesus, the true high priest. We are taught that even though His arms outstretched in blessing was a one-time act, it also revealed the everlasting attitude of His heart. As far as His heart is concerned, His arms are still stretched out in benediction toward us.

As He ascended, it is very likely that He repeated the high priestly benediction recorded in Numbers 6:24-26:

The LORD bless you, and keep you;
The LORD make His face shine on you,
And be gracious to you;
The LORD lift up His countenance on you,
And give you peace.

These words were spoken to encourage the people that God had accepted the blood of the sacrificial Lamb and that He was now favorably disposed toward them.

Can you picture the disciples watching in awe as He slowly ascended into heaven with His arms outstretched in blessing? Perhaps they saw the glory wounds in the palms of His hands as He blessed them. It was a sight God intended them to remember forever. He wanted their last view of Him to display His heart's desire to always bless them.

Praise be to the Lord, who never gets tired of blessing us in Christ Jesus.

6 God Will Reveal It

*I*f your heart is now sensitive toward the Lord and you desire to live a life that honors Him, the enemy of your soul may seek to take advantage of your tender spirit. He would rob you of your joy by convincing you that a cloud of condemnation still hovers overhead when, in fact, the sky is blue. Because you are responsive to the high call to holiness and so swift to receive conviction, you may become an easy prey to his insidious suggestions.

In determining the difference between the genuine conviction of God's Holy Spirit and the incessant nagging of the devil, there is a principle you can apply without failure. It is found in Philippians 3:15:

> Let us therefore, as many as are perfect, have this attitude; and *if*
> *in anything you have a different attitude, God will reveal that also*
> *to you.*

The disposition Paul is referring to is the attitude the Lord Jesus had when He emptied Himself, taking the form of a bond servant, in order to please the Father. The Lord has promised that if in anything you have a contrary attitude, God will be faithful to reveal it to you.

One can always discern the Holy Spirit's conviction because He is specific. If there is something in our lives that needs attention, the Lord will reveal it to us. God is not vague when He is dealing with our sin; He does not speak to us in glittering generalities so that we will have an oppressive weight of guilt pressing down upon us. No!

He identifies the problem; He puts His finger exactly on the thing that displeases Him.

Satan, on the other hand, loves to torment God's dear children. He attempts to make us feel guilty about everything. He enjoys magnifying our unworthiness, and he attempts to get us to look at ourselves apart from our union with Jesus Christ. He tries to imitate the Holy Spirit's conviction by placing us under a general cloud of guilt and condemnation. Those who are nagged by the enemy have no particular sin to confess before God. They feel guilty and unworthy but cannot identify the specific problem. In this way Satan loves to torment those who are sensitive toward God.

My friend, I encourage you to apply this wonderful promise from Philippians 3:15. If you find yourself under such a cloud, go straight to the Lord and pray according to His promise: "I am fearful I do not have the attitude of Christ. Lord, You have promised that if in anything I should have a different attitude, You would reveal it to me. If there is some specific thing that displeases You, please reveal it to me!"

If the Lord does not bring a definite conviction to your heart, rise up in the joy of the Lord and ignore the nagging of the evil one.

If you leave the precious place of prayer under a cloud, it will be the cloud of unbelief and not the cloud of guilt.

I would not deliberately say anything to discourage your sensitivity to the Lord. I only seek to disarm the enemy of the weapon he has used so effectively against God's tender lambs.

The joy of the Lord is your strength!

7 Closer to Jesus and to the Jubilee

*Y*ou may count it strange that the closer you draw to the Lord Jesus, the more other things lose their attraction to your heart. But this is exactly the truth that was graphically illustrated by the Year of Jubilee.

If a person purchased a portion of a brother's inheritance in the tenth year, he would be required to pay a large price, for he would be able to utilize the land for forty more years. If he purchased the same property in the twentieth year, it would be less expensive because he could only hold it for thirty years and the return he could receive from the land would not be as great. The closer one approached the fiftieth year, the less one would have to pay for the land. By God's command, at the Jubilee, all property would revert back to the original owner. If someone waited until the forty-eighth or forty-ninth year to purchase the property, it would be almost free because it would be in the buyer's possession for only a couple of years before it had to be returned. The closer one got to that glorious day, the more things would lose their value.

Oh, the glory of that truth! For us, Jubilee is more than being with the Lord in heaven. Although it is superlatively true that— as our any-moment death approaches or His any-moment return draws near—the things that are temporal relinquish their hold as treasures in our hearts, there is also a present application of the truth of Jubilee. As we draw near to the Lord Jesus by faith through the study of His Word, the glory of all shakable things fade, and what we once regarded as gain appears as rubbish to us.

That is why as your desire grows for Jesus, other things will not mean as much to you anymore.

I, too, am becoming disillusioned with the imaginary value of the fleeting things of this world as I draw near to the Savior. God will not share His glory with another. Others may attribute our preoccupation with Jesus to the effects of aging, but we know we are just getting closer to God's Jubilee.

May your heart ever be where He who is your treasure is!

8 The New Covenant Student of the Word

*A*re you a New Covenant student of the Word of God?

By that I do not have in mind the two great divisions of the Bible. I do not mean that a New Covenant student of the Word should study only the twenty-seven inspired books in the New Testament. When the apostle Paul expounded the New Covenant to the Corinthian Christians, there was no New Testament.

The confusion between the Old and New Covenants and the Old and New Testaments has caused some to neglect the wonderful Old Testament Scriptures. Something is terribly wrong with any approach to the Lord that encourages God's people to neglect thirty-nine books of the Bible.

And many who concentrate on the New Testament Scriptures do so with an Old Covenant heart. This is a sad thing. On the other hand, there are many who study the Old Testament Scriptures with a New Covenant heart. This is thrilling to behold.

The New Covenant student comes to all the Bible in order to behold the Lord in His glory. It may sound spiritual to say "I am coming to the Scriptures with a desire to *obey* God," but that may be a subtle indication of a legal spirit. We cannot obey God until we have beheld Him. Whether we're in the Old Testament or the New, the *heart* must study to behold the Lord.

The New Covenant approach to the written Word is many light-years away from studying merely to learn a new doctrine or truth. If we study only to glean some principle for life, some "how-to" formulas for raising a family or winning souls, or some secrets for holy living, we fall short of God's description of a New Covenant Christian. The New Covenant believer realizes that all of these excellent things will find their proper place as by-products of beholding the Lord. The one who comes to the Scriptures, humbly trusting God to reveal Himself, is a New Covenant student of the Word of God.

It is because New Covenant Christians have been delivered from self-trust and are grounded in the pure grace of God that they believe the Christian life is the fruit of beholding the Lord in the Scriptures. They are certain, if they behold Him with an unveiled face, that they will be progressively transformed into His likeness.

Prayerfully study all parts of the Bible with a New Covenant heart. The Old Testament contains the truth in seed form, profoundly illustrated by redemptive history; the New Testament presents the same truth in fully developed form. Study the Pentateuch to know God; study the historical books to behold His glory; study the poetical books with the same passion. Pray with Moses, "Show me, I pray Thee, Thy glory."

Study the prophets to behold the Savior; study the Gospels to be transformed by a vision of the Lord; study the book of Acts the same way. All the epistles reveal Him, so study to behold Him. Study the consummating Revelation to see the Lord. Be a New Covenant student of the Word of God.

Truth is a person and His lovely name is Jesus. Our deep hunger to obey the Lord will be satisfied when, in reality, we behold this Truth.

9 God's Burdens Are Prophecies

I have never been so burdened to pray," you may at times say, "yet nothing is happening!"

I assure you, if you are burdened by God to pray, then something wonderful is happening! The Lord never prompts His children to pray in vain. He would not mock us with burdens that He was not intending to lift. It is probable that the more intense the burden becomes to intercede, the greater will be the miracle when God fully answers the prayer.

Continue to pray in the Spirit, and may the Lord make you keenly sensitive to His faithful working. Unless He opens our eyes, we would never detect the finger of God.

Do you remember in 1 Kings 18 when Elijah the prophet heard with the ear of faith the roar of a heavy shower? He was burdened at that time to pray for rain. While he prayed he sent his servant to watch for the answer. Six times the servant returned with the same words, "There is nothing!" but the seventh time he reported that he had seen a cloud as small as a man's hand coming up from the sea. That cloud was the precursor of a great outpouring.

Take comfort in the fact that God has been pleased to burden you to pray; believe that the burden is, in a sense, a prophecy. You have learned to watch and pray; now pray and watch with thanksgiving. Be alert to the smallest hint that God is active. Do not allow physical sight to hinder you from spiritual expectancy. Keep looking until you have looked seven times, for in the fullness of time you will behold the seemingly insignificant cloud the size of a man's hand.

Others may dismiss that cloud as a false assurance, but by it, God will water your hope. It may be only a surprising word, an unexpected gesture, a momentary openness, some faint response to the Lord, but pray on! It is for you as it was when the Lord reminded the prophet Habakkuk: "Observe! Be astonished! Wonder! Because I am doing something in your days—you would not believe if you were told" (1:5).

We need to be numbered among those who search for the cloud. Let others conclude that God is doing nothing even though we pray. Our burden to pray is our reason to sing. Do not conclude by six futile trips to look toward the sea that the Lord is withholding rain. It will surely come! Your spirit will hear the sound of the shower before your eye sees the cloud. The seventh look cannot be far off!

10 We Wish to See Jesus

Our Lord Jesus seemed to ignore the small contingent of Greeks who came to Philip with the request, "Sir, we wish to see Jesus" (John 12:21). But this requires a second look.

Although it is true that there is no record of our Lord Jesus going out to meet these Greeks, of His inviting them in to commune with Him, or even of some messenger being sent by Him to relate some message to them of His intention, I do not think we can justly conclude that our Lord Jesus ignored or snubbed them. It would not be fair, from the evidence available to us, to charge our Lord Jesus with rudeness. In our Savior's deity He was always compassionate; in His humanity He was always a perfect gentleman.

Some take the position that the Greeks were insincere in their motives in coming, and that the Lord refused to respond to them because they sought only to behold some sign. Since no comment is given about their motives in coming, I think Christian charity must guide us to assume that their desire to see Him was honest. Others think these Greeks were ignored because the door to the Gentiles for the gospel had not yet fully opened.

I am inclined to believe that our Lord Jesus did not ignore them, but actually He answered their deepest request on the very highest level.

When their request was presented to Him, Jesus was approaching the hour of His destiny. It must have been so refreshing to His spirit to hear of some waiting outside who had a great desire to see

Him. His response to the disciples upon hearing of this desire of the Greeks is very instructive. It was at this precise moment that He gave His great discourse on the grain of wheat that had to die in order to produce much fruit.

It is as if our Lord Jesus said, "There is a group of hungry Greeks who desire to know Me! How wonderful! Then I must hasten to the cross! By this means alone can the deep cry of their hearts be met. I must be lifted up so that not only the seeking Greeks but all men may be drawn to Me. If I would truly answer them, it must not be by words. It must be by My action! They do not need an interview or a sermon. They need a Savior! I will go straightway to the cross so that their desire to see Me might be eternally satisfied."

Our Lord Jesus often leaves us standing in silence and wondering if He has ignored our petitions or disregarded our desire to behold Him. But in those confusing times we may know from this story that He is over-answering our prayer. When He is not speaking to us, He is *doing* for us.

We must be patient until the grain of wheat has been allowed to die and rise again. Then we will see the harvest of our petitions.

Our Lord never ignores those who desire to see Him. It may appear that way to blind sight, but the reality is that our God is very active in drawing all men unto Himself.

We all deserve to have Him ignore us, but He never will. When His words are few, let us be watching for His wondrous works. True seekers never stand long without His revelation.

Rest!

11 When to Stop Praying

*I*ncreasingly in my life I have found Romans 8:26 to be true: "We do not know how to pray as we should."

I am so glad that God followed up that sentence with these precious words: "But the Spirit Himself intercedes for us with groanings too deep for words."

No matter how much insight we are given on the important gift of prayer, we will never come to the place where we can pray in perfect conformity with all the will of God.

I was meditating on Abraham's wonderful prayer of intercession for his nephew Lot and his family and the five cities of the valley in the day of God's severe judgment on Sodom and Gomorrah. His prayer (in Genesis 18) was so intimate and humble as he begged God for mercy if there could be found fifty righteous people within the city. Then, remembering that he was but dust and ashes himself, he asked God to spare the cities if there were forty-five righteous ones there. In wonderful boldness, as his vision of God's merciful heart increased, he reduced the number of his request to forty, then thirty, then twenty—right down to ten. God promised our father Abraham that if ten righteous persons were found there, He would withhold His judgment.

I wondered, as I thought upon this marvelous illustration of intercession, why Abraham stopped praying at the number ten. Why didn't he continue and say, "If there are seven righteous, or five or three or one—will You then spare the city from Your holy wrath?" Abraham knew when to stop praying.

I am beginning to see the importance of knowing when to stop praying. His Spirit must guide us in this.

There is many a Moses to whom God must say, "Why are you crying out to Me? Tell the sons of Israel to go forward"…many a Joshua who must hear the words of the Lord, "Rise up! Why is it that you have fallen on your face? Israel has sinned!"…many a Samuel to whom God says, "How long will you grieve over Saul, since I have rejected him?" It feels very spiritual to keep on praying, but there is a time to stop. May God enable us to so walk in His light that we know when to pray and when to cease praying.

I hope this suggestion leads you into a deeper knowledge of Christ. May God help you to embrace His heart.

12 Delayed Answers to Long-Forgotten Prayers

*I*t would seem reasonable to regard unanswered prayer as a negative response from the Lord. If the prayer is unanswered, we assume the Lord is denying the request. A denial is not difficult to take for one who is seeking only the Lord's face and favor. To the heart that desires only the perfect will of the Lord and that the Lord receives all the glory He deserves, it is no crisis to be denied. We do not trust our own wisdom when we pray; He knows what is best for us. It is incidental to a believing heart whether God says yes or no, as long as He is honored.

However, in the full light of revelation, I am not certain that unanswered prayer is actually God's denial of the request. Consider, for example, the case of Zacharias, the father of John the Baptizer. When he received the news that his wife, Elizabeth, would bear him a son in her old age, he was standing in the temple of God on the right of the altar of incense. The angel Gabriel, who stands in the presence of God, appeared to him and greeted him (in Luke 1:13) with these words: "Do not be afraid, Zacharias, for your petition has been heard."

Zacharias responded, "I am an old man, and my wife is advanced in years." In light of that, it would appear that the prayer request Gabriel referred to had gone unanswered for many years. I wonder how many years had passed since the couple cried that request unto the Lord? I can picture them as a young married couple desiring to have a family, petitioning the Lord to open her womb so she could bear a child. As the years rolled on, however, and she did not become pregnant, they must have taken the unanswered prayer to be a no from God. It is possible, even if they had never forgotten this request made in their youth, that they would not have desired the Lord's positive answer at this late date in their lives.

I use this story to illustrate the truth that not all unanswered prayer indicates a denial from the Lord. God may delay answering our prayers—even for many years. Yet that does not necessarily mean God has forgotten what we prayed in faith. We may have long forgotten the prayers we have prayed in years past, but like the incense in the golden bowls that appeared before God's throne in eternity, our prayers are always present before God.

Delayed prayer is not forgotten prayer. We may trust the Lord for His perfect timing.

If God means no, then He will make it very clear. We would be wise not to be too swift to interpret God's silence as His refusal. God is ever working toward eternity, and that takes time.

Keep praying! The great miracle, after all, is not the answer to prayer but the fact that God has allowed us to communicate with Him at all. Prayer is the miracle!

Let us keep our eyes alert to God's answers to our long-forgotten prayers.

13   Expect God to Over-Answer Prayer

Although it is true that we will never get beyond Romans 8:26—"We do not know how to pray as we should"—yet there are some glorious things revealed about prayer that we can know with deep assurance.

You will be delighted to meditate on the truth of Ephesians 3:20-21:

> Now to Him who is able to do exceeding abundantly beyond all
> that we ask or think, according to the power that works within
> us, to Him be the glory in the church and in Christ Jesus to all
> generations forever and ever. Amen.

The apostle Paul penned this great benediction that we might glorify God for the fact that He always over-answers the prayers of His children. He gives not from His bounty but according to the riches of His glory. If you or I were to give out of our finite store, we would become poorer by giving. Even if we gave only a little, our resources would be diminished by that much. The more we drew from our accounts, the less we would have. Every gift would have to be subtracted from our wealth until eventually we would become impoverished by our generosity.

The Lord gives according to His infinite riches. The Lord is as rich after He gives as He was before He gave. His supply of forgiveness or grace or strength or patience does not get smaller and smaller as His children receive from His hand. We need never fear that what we ask from Him is in short supply.

This requires that His giving transcend our asking. Paul adds one modifier after another to drive home this wonderful truth to the hearts of praying saints. "God is able to do *all* we ask," he says. Not just *what* we ask, but *all* we ask. If Paul had stopped there we would bless God forever, but he also says, "*beyond* all we ask." Then to underscore God's wonderful heart Paul adds, "*abundantly* beyond all we ask." Even then he did not stop, but under the inspiration of the Holy Spirit tells us that it is "*exceeding* abundantly beyond all we ask." Just when we think we've come to the end of God's promise, Paul adds the words, "all we ask *or think.*"

Oh, the glory of these words: *exceeding abundantly beyond all we ask or think.* How amazing! God's giving exceeds all of our puny requests and wildest imaginations.

I believe we are too modest in our praying. If we were speaking of anyone other than our infinite God, I would dismiss such language as poetic hyperbole, but because God is who He is, it is literally true that He over-answers all our prayers.

May God teach us to pray to the outer limits of our vocabulary and to the outer limits of our imaginations. When we have requested all that our capacities can conceive, then let us expect Him to over-answer.

Not only will God answer prayer in His own time and way; He will over-answer in His own time and way.

I am sure the reality of this can be applied to all prayer, but it was given in terms of Paul's prayer that the Ephesian believers be filled with all the fullness of God. If He over-answers that request, heaven cannot be far off.

14 Abba

C hildlikeness is the mark of maturity. Oh, that God's people would embrace the Lord in such a way that the Spirit of Adoption would be manifest in their lives!

Abba—three times in the New Testament (Mark 14:36; Romans 8:15; Galatians 4:6) the Holy Spirit uses that precious word to illustrate our wonderful dependence upon and union with the Savior. It is almost impossible to translate this word selected by the Holy Spirit to so wonderfully describe our childlike disposition toward the Lord. It is the child's prattle. It is best expressed by our English word *DaDa*. It is the first uttering of the infant as he looks, with arms outstretched, to his father bending over him to lift him up. "DaDa," says the baby.

For years I was profoundly moved by the intensity of the suffering of the Lord Jesus in the Garden of Gethsemane. His agony was so intense. He cried out with a loud voice, and He sweat, as it were, great drops of blood. But there is something else in the Garden of Gethsemane as awesome as the intensity of His sorrow. When He asked His Father if it was possible to remove the cup from Him, He began His request with the words *Abba, Father.*

Exactly one day before He would accomplish death and redemption on the cross, He looked up into the face of His Father, and in the agony of His soul He said, "DaDa."

O my friend, the indignity of those hours is forever past, and now our Lord is exalted at the Father's right hand. He has sent the

Spirit of God into our hearts, crying in us, and causing us to cry, "Abba, Father." That is the Spirit of Adoption. That is the childlike mark of maturity. That is the manifestation of our union with Him.

I know of nothing more wonderful than the fact that the Holy Spirit in my heart is crying out utterances of childlike dependence through me. He did not come into my heart crying, "Local Church," "Missions," "Discipleship," "Ministry," or "Spiritual Gifts"; He came into my heart crying, "Abba, Father!" God poured His life into me, and that very life cries out for more of His life.

Since the Holy Spirit is ever praying that we realize the depths of our sonship and adoption, we may draw near to Him in childlike familiarity and trust. May this evidence of maturity mark our lives evermore.

15 Any Plan Will Do

*I*f you are raising a family, there is much wise counsel in the pages of Christian literature that will be helpful in all stages of your parenting experience. But I cannot recommend one parenting plan over another for you to follow. Whether you decide to follow plan A or plan B, or to combine them both with plan C, the important thing is to be certain that you have the blessing of the Lord. It is His blessing that makes one rich without sorrow.

In Psalm 127, wise Solomon reminded us:

> Unless the LORD builds the house,
> They labor in vain who built it;
> Unless the LORD guards the city,
> The watchman keeps awake in vain.

We are by nature builders, and by nature we seek to protect that which we have built. Whether we are building a friendship, a business, a ministry, a reputation, a relationship, or a family, we must finally ask, "Does this building have the blessing of the Lord?" If it does not, how wasted are the energy and resources that have been poured into the construction.

I am sure you will not lack the advice of loved ones who long to see you succeed in all that lies before you as a parent. One will recommend one plan; another will propound the advantages of another. It can be overwhelming! But any plan will work if you are trusting the Lord and not the plan; no plan will succeed, no matter how excellent, if it does not have the blessing of the Lord upon it.

Choose a plan and trust Jesus. He is the Builder of the house, and the glory of the house belongs to Him. The same would be true as you choose a strategy to guard and protect those under your care. Many plans and advice abound, but unless the Lord guards the city, the watchmen keep awake in vain. As the building of the family ultimately depends upon the Lord, so does the defense of the family. He must be the Guard of the city. All precaution is in vain without the blessing of the Lord.

We must carefully choose the most secure environment to shelter our tender lambs from wolves, but their true security depends upon the Lord and not upon our carefully chosen defenses.

I am not at all suggesting that you lay down your responsibilities in building or guarding. I am simply pointing you to the higher principle of trusting the Lord so you don't build or guard in vain.

Choose a plan to build and trust the Lord; choose a plan to guard and trust the Lord. Any plan will do if you have the blessing of the Lord. Relax and believe God. As you look at that bundle of needs and think of all the building and protecting that must be accomplished, remember that Jesus is the Builder of the house and the Defender of the city. All vigilance, without faith in Him, is vain.

Do not run after the right plan. Run hard after the Lord who desires to bless your family.

16 God Wants Us to Be Ourselves

*I*n the past I have become engrossed in reading Christian biography. I coveted the spiritual experiences I read, and I vainly thought that by imitating their methods I could recreate their experiences in my own life. I attempted to *be* them. I was willing to sacrifice my own identity to receive what they had received from God.

The Lord teaches us the safe way to study Christian biography in Hebrews 11–12. He bids us meditate on the experiences of men and women of faith, then He turns our eyes away from them and their faith and invites us to look unto the Lord Jesus, the Author and Finisher of faith.

Jacob greatly desired to be blessed by his father, Isaac, and he thought that by disguising himself as his older brother, Esau, he could guarantee the blessing. Oh, the bitter experiences he endured because he was willing to sacrifice his own identity to take on the identity of his brother to receive blessing!

May your heart be greatly challenged and your faith encouraged by the lives of those you read about, but do not cease to be yourself. God desires to be Himself in terms of who *you* are. Learn swiftly, as young David learned, that Saul's sword and armor were made for Saul. It was very cumbersome for David. David had to trust the Lord in terms of his own personality. If God has prepared a sword and armor for you, a sling and stone will never do; if, on the other hand, He has prepared a sling and a stone for you, you must not reach for the sword or attempt to wear the armor.

Let us read with thanksgiving about the faithfulness of our dear Lord in the lives of His children. Let us marvel at the great variety of God's ways with His own. After we have considered the faith of the brothers and sisters whom God has been pleased to use, let us look far away from their lives and from their faith to the grand object of their faith—the Lord Jesus Christ.

May the Lord stimulate you through any biographies of the saints you choose to read, and may He give you one of your own!

Rest!

17 Letting God Choose

*I*f you have a supernatural indifference to the coin of this world, and if your contentment is in Christ Jesus, you bear a powerful testimony to those who, for greed's sake, would seek to take advantage of your selfless love.

On the level of worldly wisdom, it appears in Genesis 13 that Abraham, for the sake of peace in the family, delegated the decisions of his inheritance to the choice of his nephew Lot. It reads as if Abraham was saying, "I do not want strife in the family! I am willing to take the leftovers. You make the choice and I will submit. You go your way, and I will go mine!"

But those are not the spiritual facts of the case. Abraham did not let Lot choose for him; he let God choose for him. Lot was only the instrument of the Lord. Abraham did not say, "You go your way, and I will go mine!" He said, "You go your way, and I will go God's way!" It is so satisfying to read of Abraham's faith regarding the physical inheritance. Lot was making decisions based on the pleasures his physical eye could observe, but how soon would his inheritance be reduced to ashes!

Abraham, by faith, laid down his many rights and was content with what fell to him in peace. Abraham was willing to receive the dregs, but the record shows that he did not receive the dregs. "Lift up your eyes and look from the place where you are," the Lord said to Abraham right after his separation from Lot. "Look...northward and southward and eastward and westward." Abraham, by trusting the

Lord and being willing to be exploited, was actually blessed in every direction.

I encourage you to press closely to God's heart. He will make you content with His choices for your life. He will bless you in every direction of the compass, because you have left the decisions to Him.

Through all of this, those around you may see where your heart is by observing the treasures you desire.

Show yourself to be a true child of Abraham.

Rest!

18 Christ at Home in Our Hearts

*P*erhaps Paul's prayer in Ephesians 3:17 has puzzled you. He is requesting that Christ would dwell in the hearts of his readers by faith, when it is clear from the context of the letter that they were already believers in the Lord Jesus Christ. If Christ were already indwelling His people, why would Paul pray that Christ would dwell in their hearts by faith?

The prayer of the apostle seems to be touching something very wonderful for the believer. This is not a surface prayer where a cosmetic change is requested, but a very earnest prayer that God would accomplish a profound thing in the hearts of His own. Those who have studied the Greek language tell us that the word selected by the apostle Paul for *dwell* literally means "to settle down in a dwelling." The prayer of the apostle was that Christ could feel at home in the hearts of His people.

Wouldn't it be a wonderful thing if the Lord Jesus felt the liberty to settle down and be completely at home in your heart and mine? If I may apply expressions without being irreverent, I would say that Jesus wants the freedom in our hearts to kick off His shoes, lie back in a comfortable chair, raise His feet to the table, and relax.

That is the desire that the apostle Paul expressed in this prayer for his friends. Paul had no doubt that the Lord Jesus was already residing in the hearts of the Ephesian Christians, but his prayer was that Christ might be able to dwell in peace where He was already residing.

What a wonderful prayer! How precious to think that God would actually honor such a prayer and respond by causing His children to realize how comfortable He is in their hearts.

Perhaps one way He would begin to answer that prayer would be to work toward the absence of all the things that would militate against a comfortable dwelling of the Lord Jesus in our hearts. A few moments of meditation would instruct us on the kind of place that would *not* make God comfortable. We know what displeases Him. He would have to create for us a house that is clean and free of tension and anxiety. He would relax in a heart that was relaxed and serene. Oh, for a holy and peaceful house where God would be comfortable!

I desire this prayer to be answered in my life—that Jesus would *dwell* where He already lives! That He would relax where He resides! That He could enjoy communion in the place He inhabits!

Let us pray this prayer for ourselves and for one another. Let us do more and apply the prayer corporately, praying that Christ would be completely at home in our fellowship and assemblies.

Rest! Enjoy! Worship!

WHEN I AM AFRAID...

1 Sufficient Grace for the Perfect Time

*I*f you fear failing the Lord in the day of severe testing, your fear is groundless, for you are reasoning from the wrong side of grace. To suffering people, God gives grace to suffer; to dying people, He gives grace to die. It is because you are neither suffering nor dying that you do not yet have the grace that you would need if you were.

Be assured that the Lord will support you in the very hour you need Him. We must not give glory to the martyrs who died courageously and honored God with their parting sighs. They were simple Christians who were supplied from the Lord in their hour of testing. All our springs are in the Lord, and He will meet our need when the time is perfect.

I believe this truth is wonderfully illustrated in the life of the great apostle Paul. When he penned the letter to the Philippians, he was in prison awaiting word as to whether he would live or die. A strong possibility existed that he would be called upon to suffer a violent death for the sake and name of his Lord Jesus. His letter spoke of an earnest expectation and hope. He believed he would be able to submit boldly and shamelessly to suffering and death; he had the conviction that he would actually glorify God in the process, because he had every expectation that the Lord would provide the necessary grace when he needed it. Paul did not say, "I have what it takes to die

95

a martyr's death" No! He said, "I have an earnest expectation and hope that by the time I need it, I will have what it takes."

When a person speaks of an expectation and hope, he does not yet possess the thing he desires. It is in prospect. It is in the future. Paul had an overwhelming confidence in the Lord that, by the time he needed grace to suffer or die for Jesus, it would be available to him. He had experienced the great faithfulness of the Lord throughout his life as a Christian, and always the Lord had been there for him. Every time he required more grace, more grace was supplied.

If you could have candidly spoken with Paul in his prison cell as he waited for the word of his possible execution, I believe he would have said something like this: "I am naturally as chicken-hearted as you are when it comes to suffering for Jesus. I cannot imagine that I will do well when that time comes. But I don't live by what I imagine; I live by what I know. Although I do not have what it takes, I do have, living in my heart, *who* it takes. He can create in me all I need to support me in that hour. I fully expect He will provide all-sufficient grace to enable me to bear all things victoriously. The only thing I have for the present moment is expectation and hope. Suitable grace to honor Jesus will surely be granted when it is needed and not before."

We must not reason on the wrong side of grace. The Lord does not portion grace to us before it is needed. The greater the need, the greater the grace will be.

It may sound humble to think that we would not be able to suffer for Jesus, but I fear it is the thinking of unbelief. You and I have the Lord and, with Him, the same earnest expectation and hope that the apostle had.

Whatever we may face in our future, the Lord will be there to supply us with sufficient grace. Until we need it, let us rest in the expectation and the hope.

May Paul's confession help us think God's thoughts and see things through God's eyes.

2 He Always Provides for Our True Needs

*H*ave you asked the Lord to fulfill all your needs? This mighty request requires no intercession from others, for God *will* provide for *all* of your needs in Christ Jesus without their asking Him to do so. He is your heavenly Father, and as such, He has obligated Himself to meet your necessities.

Any anxiety we have concerning temporal necessities issues from unbelief. We need never worry about what we shall eat, drink, or wear. These things our Father knows we need, and so we must not fret about them as do those who are not in living union with the Lord.

The reality is that if I do not have something, I do not need it. God is meeting all of my needs at every moment. The Lord is my Shepherd, I shall not lack. That is always true.

I believe the confusion comes because we do not know what our true needs really are. We can ask the Lord in a general way to give us our daily bread, but what is our daily bread? Isaiah reminds us that for a season the Lord fed His people with the bread of affliction because of their special need. Peter wrote to afflicted Christian pilgrims and reminded them that their heaviness in manifold temptations was necessary for the testing of their faith. Peter said, "If need be" God would allow them to experience trouble and affliction.

God is always meeting the needs of all of His children. We do not know what our needs are, and so we must ever trust Him to supply the things we need as He sees and understands them.

If I need bread, He will provide bread. If I need poverty, He is also faithful to provide poverty. I may think I need deliverance from a certain thing, but God knows it is more needful for me to know Him through struggle, so He allows the conflict to continue to meet my greater need. If we are in need of patience, what do you suppose God may allow in our lives? If we are in need of Calvary love, do you think He may send some unlovely persons our way so we can learn to appropriate His love?

Any suggestion that God is not at all times providing for our every need fosters discontent. That does not mean we should judge the hearts of those who feel a burden to share a list of supposed needs in an attempt to enlist the prayer support of the body. We should rather encourage them to remember that God is meeting their needs before they ask.

What a hallowed rest is ours, abiding in the Father's care! We must not wrong His faithfulness by needless fretting. As long as God remains, our waters are sure; the same love that prompts the Lord to lavish His supply on us in times of necessity induces Him to withhold it. That is His business. Ours is to trust.

If we were alive to our real needs and how He ever meets them, we would never stop blessing God for what a supplier He is. Peace finds its footing in the character of God.

Rest!

3 Safety

When is a Christian in the most spiritual danger? The very simple answer is, When the eyes of the heart are taken off the Lord Jesus as the object of faith.

Every place is safe for a Christian if the Lord is embraced and trusted; no place is safe if union with Christ is disregarded and the believer leans upon human wisdom or strength. Fellowship with the Lord Jesus can secure the heart, even if duty calls it through the very flames of hell. Our safety is ever His keeping grace that is appropriated by childlike faith.

If that same question is more directed at personal application to the circumstances of life, I answer, "The lonely place and the high place are especially dangerous, even for the most instructed Christian."

The lonely place is dangerous because it appears to be a safe place. One might think that in solitude the heart would be more apt to draw near to the Lord. It seems logical to assume that the fewer the distractions, the easier it would be to concentrate on Him. It may not be necessarily so. It was in the wilderness that the enemy attempted to undo the Son of God. It appears to have been far safer for the soul of Lot and his family to be vexed in Sodom than to fall into temptation and sin on some lonely mountain.

God has created and redeemed us for society, and it is in the communion of saints that we are the most secure. There may be times in the will of God when, by a choice not our own, we are banished to some lonely Patmos. If that is the case, then the Lord will surely manifest Himself to us and keep us. However, when the enemy's legion seeks to drive us to the desert, it is probably for a malicious reason. He finds an advantage, as Amalek did, in attacking the stragglers who are detached from the safety of the body, when they are in a lonely place. As a general rule, the lonely place is a dangerous place for a Christian to be.

The high place is also a dangerous place. It was on the pinnacle of the temple where Satan tried to tempt the Savior. It is on the high plain of spiritual elevation, when saints below are looking up to us and expecting from us some display of faith or courage, that we are in danger of a great fall. Oh, that is a frightful place! Pride at all times goes before destruction, but it is especially destructive when it is spiritual pride. If our Lord Jesus had yielded to the suggestion of the enemy (mad thought!) and leaped from the dizzy height, even though He were rescued by angels and brought safely to the earth, He would have been defeated. As far as God's redemptive purposes were concerned, His deliverance from falling would not have been His victory.

My friend in Christ, it is a dreadful thing to be admired by saints and rescued by angels and still to be defeated. God may rescue us from our presumption, and yet we may be ruined as far as His original intention for our lives is concerned. Although the Christian community applauds us for our demonstration of faith, what is gained if the heart of our Savior is grieved? What a tragic undoing of a spiritual life!

God can and often does keep our feet in high places and give us the surefootedness of the hind. However, we must ever make sure we have clear direction from Him and proceed with prayerful caution when we attempt to ascend the high seat.

Our safety is to walk in union with Jesus. Our wisdom is to walk in union with Jesus in the blessed company of the saints. Our safety and wisdom is to walk in union with Jesus, in the communion of saints, in the lowliness of a bondslave of Jesus.

May God keep us there!

4 The Finger of God

*A*t the moment you may be very sensitive to the power of the enemy in your life. Please do not allow your determination to escape entrapment distract you from focusing on the Lord Jesus. Your Best Friend is your victorious warrior. We must not be caught looking at our vulnerabilities or at Satan's schemes. Our only safeguard from the enemy is to be consumed with the Lord Jesus Christ Himself.

In light of that truth, what does Jesus mean by the phrase *the finger of God* in Luke 11:20? He said, "If I cast out demons *by the finger of God,* then the kingdom of God has come upon you."

In Matthew 12:28, we have another record of the same event. Under the inspiration of the Holy Spirit, Matthew writes, "If I cast out demons *by the Spirit of God,* then the kingdom of God has come upon you."

The expression *the finger of God* is interchangeable with the expression *the Spirit of God.*

When God gave Moses the law, written on the two tablets of stone on Mount Sinai, we read that God's law was "written by the finger of God" (Exodus 31:18). It was the Spirit of the living God that burned God's holy law into those tablets.

When Jannes and Jambres, the magicians of Egypt who opposed Moses, confessed "This is the finger of God," they were admitting that they could not imitate the mighty works of God by trickery, because these were actually being done by the Spirit of God.

Your victory must come by the finger of God. The finger of God is the Spirit of God, and the Spirit of God is the very life of God. By the life of God you may daily triumph over everything and everyone that dares oppose the work of the Lord in your life.

Is not the finger of God an apt description of the blessed Holy Spirit? It reminds us at once of the mighty power of the One whose work it is and the ease with which He does it. In Psalm 8 the heavens are said to be the work of God's fingers. We know it was with the ease of omnipotence that God created the heavens. It is comforting to know that the same finger of God is engaged in our defense.

His fingerprint clearly marks your life. Let us, by His finger, press on to victory!

5 Sarah: Mother of Faith

S arah, by faith, called Abraham, "lord." It is true that the only record we have of her using those very words is in connection with God's promise to her that she would deliver a baby. In stunned unbelief she said to Abraham, "Shall I have pleasure, *my lord*, being old also?" (Genesis 18:12).

If that is the occasion when she was credited in 1 Peter 3 for her faith, then we have much reason to rejoice, for we know the good Lord must comb through every sentence of ours in order to find something in it to reward. If indeed that is the occasion Peter refers to, then within her sentence of doubt and disbelief she used a term of respect for her husband, and the Lord gave her credit for being submissive to Abraham.

But I wonder if that is the story Peter had in mind when he chose Sarah to become the illustration of the mother of faith. Peter describes her as an example of having faith in "the hidden person of the heart." By this act of faith, whatever it was, Sarah has become the mother of faith and all that follow her example are called children of Sarah.

I think the context of 1 Peter 3 suggests a different story from the life of Sarah. The chapter begins with Peter, under the inspiration of the Holy Spirit, teaching wives to submit to their husbands even if their husbands should be disobedient to the Word of God. He reminds us of the awesome power and influence of the submissive wife, even if she does not utter a single word. It is possible that Sarah called Abraham "lord" with her life rather than with her lips. More than once she called him lord by her godly behavior—by her silent submission. Her submission to her husband said, "Abraham is lord!"

It is possible that Peter is referring to a time when Abraham was not responding to Sarah as the husband God intended him to be. Abraham, in fear for his own life, twice placed his dear wife in a dangerous situation by presenting her to the heathen as his sister rather than his wife. It was only by the intervening miracle of God that her purity was preserved. These events would provide the background for the illustration and enforce the wonderful point Peter is making.

Sarah, in that dreadful situation, showed a sacrificial love for her husband. Peter not only calls attention to the fact that she submitted to him by her actions, calling him lord, but he adds, "She hoped in God." Oh, how she must have prayed that night that she would not be violated by the hands of the ungodly. By her trust in the Lord to protect her even when her human lord failed, she received the honor of becoming the mother of all those who hope in God to fight their battles for them. Sarah did more than silently submit to those in authority over her. She hoped in God. No doubt she had natural fears, but Peter tells us that she was not frightened by them. What a paradox! It is no wonder that such a life has the power to win over those who are privileged to behold it.

Every time we submit to those in authority over us and trust the Lord to fight our battles (leaving the consequences to Him), we prove ourselves to be the children of Sarah.

How swift we are to raise our hand in our own defense! How slow to hope in God! How unwilling we are to submit, especially when those in authority over us are clearly acting in disobedience to the Word!

May God increase Sarah's family.

6 The Cure for Our Anxiety

*D*o you desire to be rid of anxiety forever? I can identify with that desire. I have been anxious about my anxiety. This is the common yearning of the whole body of the Savior. In this pilgrim walk, we all sing from the same hymnal. Shame on us for fretting and worrying about the fading things of life when we have such a wonderful heavenly Father who knows that we have material needs and who has never failed in providing those needs for us.

In Luke's record of the great discourse of the Lord Jesus on the essence and characteristics of the life that has finally settled on Christ as its only treasure, the good doctor turns our eyes to the lordship of Christ. In Luke 12, Jesus shows us the foolishness and needlessness of greed and anxiety.

Our real life does not consist in the things of this world, so we should not pursue them as if they could bring us contentment. We know we should not be anxious about how material things will be provided for us. But how are we delivered from greed on the one hand and from anxiety on the other?

God invites us to "seek first His kingdom and His righteousness." He reminds us that it is His good pleasure to give us the kingdom. He turns our eyes completely away from this world, from all the things for which we naturally tend to grasp and over which we needlessly worry, unto the King and His kingdom.

What is a kingdom? It is a sphere of rule over which a king rules. It is the part of the domain over which the king has dominion. The king doesn't say, "Stop worrying!" He says, "Seek first the kingdom!" We are invited to set our hearts on Christ as our Lord and treasure, and we are assured that our hearts will soon abide where our treasure is.

The cure for anxiety is not quitting anxiety; the cure for anxiety is the lordship of Jesus. Just so, the cure for greed is not a determination to lay aside the inordinate desires, but rather an embracing of Jesus Christ as Lord.

When the Lord Jesus reigns in an unfettered way in our lives, we are at rest.

I fear that if you try to fight anxiety, it will only become worse. It certainly became worse in my case.

Let us gladly bow before the Lord Jesus and grant Him the crown rights in our lives, and all the things that fan our needless fretting will be added unto us.

The way to stop worrying about our worrying is to look to the Lord Jesus. When He becomes our preeminent treasure, our hearts will be delivered from all the things that unsettle us and we will dwell where He is.

May these words strum a chord or two in your heart.

WHEN I HAVE DOUBTS...

1 The Godly Sometimes Doubt

A righteous person is not one who never falls, but one who, after falling, rises up again. Seven times, says the writer of Proverbs, will the righteous fall. The number seven undoubtedly indicates that there will never be a time, short of heaven, when the Christian will be sanctified beyond the possibility of falling. But the believer differs from the nonbeliever in that, by the grace of God, the righteous will rise after every fall; the ungodly fall and stay down.

Just as a righteous person is not one who never falls, so a believing person is not one who never doubts but knows what to do when doubts arise in the heart.

John the Baptizer is an illustration of a believer who found himself suddenly encompassed with doubts. In the face of overwhelming evidence to the contrary, John came to a melancholy day in his life when, from his prison cell, he vented the question, "Is this the Christ or should we seek for another?"

We are very surprised to find a man with John's spiritual history cumbered so with doubt. What stories his parents must have told him of the visit of the angel Gabriel to them and the circumstances of his own miraculous birth! John saw many people repent and turn to the Lord; he saw the Heavenly Dove descend and abide upon his cousin, the Lord Jesus; he knew in his heart that Jesus was the sacrificial Lamb that would die for the sins of the world. John rejoiced greatly when people stopped following him and began to follow the

Savior. All he ever sought was the increase of Jesus—but now doubts upset his perfect rest. Although Jesus once described John as the opposite of a reed shaken in the wind, nevertheless, the spiritual eye can see his faith begin to waver in the strong winds of his difficult circumstances.

I believe there are at least two things that created doubts in John's heart. First of all, Jesus did not meet the expectations of John. John believed that Messiah would come with a fan and a fire: a fan to winnow the wheat and a fire to incinerate the chaff. John expected Jesus to reveal Himself in severity, but Jesus came in tenderness and sympathetic love; He ministered to the oppressed and the spiritually hungry. John's imperfect vision and expectation of how Jesus should act created doubts in his heart.

Second, John doubted because Jesus did not rescue him and deliver him from his terrible circumstances. The Messiah was anointed by the Spirit of God to proclaim the year of spiritual jubilee. He was to announce liberty to the prisoner. Where was deliverance for John? John was imprisoned for righteousness' sake, and Jesus didn't lift a finger to rescue him. Jesus taught His disciples that the sick and the prisoner should be visited. Where was Jesus? Not once had He come to visit while John was in prison. Where was the encouragement? Where was the sweet fellowship? Because John had his own expectations of how Jesus should act, and because Jesus, for His own mysterious reasons, left John unvisited in his terrible circumstances, John began to doubt.

Godly people sometimes doubt, especially when they find themselves in some lonely and dark dungeon and the Lord seems detached and far away. When expectations are disappointed and deliverance is denied, doubts abound and flourish.

But what did John do with his doubts? (Oh, how we must learn from this man who, for a brief spell, fell into questions.) He sent his doubts to Jesus. He sent an embassy to the Lord from the midst of his circumstances, which poured out John's doubts at the feet of the Savior.

It is true, the godly sometimes fall; it is also true that the godly sometimes doubt. When they fall, by grace, they rise again; when they doubt, they send their doubts to Jesus.

When I look at the answer the Lord Jesus gave to His troubled cousin, I wonder how it could have relieved his doubts. It seemed so indirect, so vague, so mysterious. However, it was the perfect answer for John's heart. It was sufficient for him.

Do not despair, my friend, because you have entertained doubts, even after you have seen so much of the Lord in your life. Send your doubts in haste to Jesus. He will satisfy your heart. His answer may not make sense to anyone else, but it will be a healing balm for you.

Doubts sent to Jesus are a great part of faith. May the Lord make a heaven of your prison. You have all the marks of a godly man. Do what the godly do—send those doubts to Jesus.

2 For Full Credit of Faith

*I*n the light of the historical record, how could the apostle Paul say of Abraham that "he did not waver in unbelief" (Romans 4:20)? It does seem puzzling to human wisdom that this seems to contradict the Genesis record. It appears that Abraham struggled much in his faith while he waited for God to fulfill His promise. Didn't he waver when he first laughed at the suggestion that his wife would bear a child in her old age, or when he desired that his servant Eliezer would become the fulfillment of the promise, or when, at Sarah's suggestion, he took Hagar into his tent in an attempt to assist the Lord? How could Paul say that Abraham was "fully assured" that God would do what He had promised, or describe him as "without being weak in faith"? Certainly we must believe that there is not a contradiction between the Old Testament record and the New Testament commentary of the same event.

A careful reading of the Genesis record reveals that God did not give Abraham all the information at one time. In fact, God allowed Abraham to walk in a very dim light.

When God first gave Abraham the promise of a seed, all that Abraham really knew about the promise, was that God intended to make of him a great nation, which would result in worldwide blessing. The second time God spoke, Abraham learned that his seed would possess the land of Canaan. When God spoke a third time, Abraham learned that his seed would be numbered as the dust of the earth. At this point in time, however, it was not certain to Abraham whether the seed would be his natural child or if Sarah would be the mother. When Abraham suggested that the Lord choose Eliezer of Damascus as the promised heir, he was not wavering in unbelief. He was living up to all the light that he had been given.

It wasn't until after Abraham's suggestion about Eliezer that God informed him that the seed would come forth from his own body. Now he knew from heaven that he would be the natural father of the seed that would become a nation to bring a blessing to every family on the earth; he knew the seed would inherit the land of Canaan and would be numbered as the dust and the stars.

Even though we are often very critical because Abraham relied on the flesh when he entered into a marriage relationship with Hagar, the fact is, he did not violate any of the light he had been given by God. He was not yet informed that Sarah would be the mother of the child. Abraham lived up to all of the light God gave him.

No one can doubt that he made many mistakes, but he did not violate light. Every time God spoke, Abraham believed God. There is a precious principle of life connected with this. When believers walk in the light that God has given them, they are given full credit for faith. When they obey what they know to be God's revealed will, God writes of them, "They wavered not...being fully assured." We may think we are stumbling all over the place and are very weak in faith; we may be sorrowfully bearing the consequences of taking Hagar into our tents; yet God judges us only by the light He has given to us.

Aren't you glad that God is not the critic that man is? I'm sure Abraham would be as surprised to read what the apostle Paul wrote about him as we are. I think Abraham would be the first to confess that he had wavering faith, but God has spoken differently.

We are not called to do everything right; we are called to walk in the light as He is in the light. Will it not be exciting to hear God's commentary on our faith and lives? I think we will be happy with celestial joy, to hear God describe the faith we had.

3 When the Purse Is Returned

A friend recently made a note to me, saying, "I think it would be easier to trust the Lord if He took away from me all visible means of support." I wonder if my friend thought carefully through that statement. Is there not a more precious evidence of true faith than being stripped of the purse?

When our Lord Jesus sent out His twelve disciples two by two in many directions and gave them authority over disease and unclean spirits, He instructed them not to carry a purse. They were not to acquire gold or silver or copper for their money belts, nor were they to carry a bag for their journey. In other words, they were to completely trust the Lord Jesus to meet all of their material needs. They were to carry no visible means of support. Without a job, a purse, or money, they were to place their faith in the Lord.

When they returned, our Lord Jesus asked them this question (in Luke 22:35): "When I sent you out without purse and bag and sandals, you did not lack anything, did you?"

They answered, "No, nothing!" They saw God supply all of their material needs even though they did not have a visible means of support. They learned through that experience how faithful the Lord was and how He could command the blessing from heaven through a great variety of means.

Then Jesus said, "But now, let him who has a purse take it along, likewise also a bag."

He returned the purse! By returning the purse, He was not saying, "You have seen God provide when you did not have a purse. Now, provide for yourself!" No! He was saying, "You have seen My faithfulness. You have begun to learn that it is I who provide for you. I proved it when you had no visible means of support. Now that you have learned that reality, I am returning your purse. I want you to live by faith even though you have a purse. Your provision comes from Me, not your purse! Can you trust Me even though you can see the purse that contains your supply?"

When a person does not have a purse (a regular source of income), it is easy to live by faith. It is very obvious who is doing the providing. It must come from the Lord. On the other hand, when a person has a purse—a productive job, the interest from wise investments, or some other independent resource of supply—and that person lives by faith—that is a sight to behold. When a brother or a sister must labor long days and full weeks to provide for the necessities of his family, and yet they can bow the head in adoring gratitude at the end of the day, knowing that all provision has come from the Lord, that is real faith. To trust God when we have a purse is a far greater evidence of faith than when we trust Him when there is no purse.

Our flesh is more easily impressed with those who minister to the Lord without a purse, but the spiritual eye beholds the saint who humbly blesses God for His faithful supply through the purse.

If God wills to remove our purse, we need never fear, for He will supply all of our needs. If, however, the Lord allows us to have a purse, we must never for a lonely moment forget that He is still the Source of all our benedictions.

With or without a purse, may we be found daily trusting Him.

4 Wrong by Faith

When the Lord enlarges our feet under us, when He brings us into a large place, when He gives us feet like the hind, He does it so that our walk with Him will be secure and not precarious. The Christian is not expected to be constantly balancing on a high wire, fearful every moment of a terrible fall. To those who love the world, the path of the Christian may be narrow, but for those of us who love the Lord, it is as boundless as the righteousness of God.

His yoke is easy. His burden is light. His commandments are delightful! The liberty we enjoy in the Lord does not encourage us to live recklessly, nor does the knowledge of His grace promote sin. We can rest confident in His promise to keep us; we need not be anxious that we will continually misstep.

But what if we are wrong? What if we are afraid to act until we know for certain we have His light?

We are instructed by the Savior to be certain that the light that is in us is not darkness after all, but we must not stumble into unbelief every time we examine our light. We must trust God as we walk in the light He has given us.

Allow me to share an illustration from the life of Abraham, the father of faith. Abraham was severely tested in his faith when he made his way up Mount Moriah to obey the Lord and to offer up his only son, Isaac, as a whole burnt offering to the Lord. He may well have asked, "But what if I am wrong?" There is no doubt that Abraham had many reasons to be confused as to what was true light and what was darkness. The command he received seemed to contradict what He knew of the character of God. Would the Lord instruct him to sacrifice his only child? How did that command square with the promise God had given earlier, which announced that Isaac's seed would bring a blessing to the world? Doesn't having a seed imply that Isaac would, some day, have to be married? Do not the facts that Isaac would one day grow up, get married, and have children imply that he would be alive to do those things?

It is interesting to note that the reasonings of Abraham's mind are not recorded for us in the book of Genesis where the record of his obedience is recorded, but rather in the book of Hebrews in the New Testament. The writer of Hebrews informs us about what was going through Abraham's mind as he made his way with his son toward the altar. Abraham reasoned, "God has promised me that my son Isaac would grow up, get married, and have children, and that eventually the entire world would be blessed through his seed. He has also commanded me to offer him up as a burnt offering. It must be, because I know that He can neither lie nor fail, that He is planning to raise up my son from the hot ashes after I have taken his life and burned his body on the altar. I will act in obedience to His command. I will obey God, and God will raise my son from the dead."

That was Abraham's reasoning. Was he correct? Was that really God's plan? Is that how it was to happen? No. Abraham was wrong, but he was wrong by faith. God honored him for believing with the limited light he had. Abraham passed the test. He was not afraid to act on the mysterious light he had been given.

When we are wrong by faith, God will always intervene for us. We do not need to be timid to walk in the light we have, even if that light is only twilight. We are not claiming infallibility; we must trust the Lord and not our light. Abraham was rewarded for being wrong, because he reasoned in faith. The issue is always, Do we trust Him?

I do not want you to be delayed in your obedience to the Lord because your light is dim. Trust the Lord and go forward in the light you have. Do not fear being wrong; fear only the possibility that you are not walking by faith. If you are wrong by faith, then you are very safe.

I write this so that you might enjoy the joy of obedience.

5 Twelve Hours in a Day

*T*he revealed will of God for us will never be at odds with our responsibilities in the Lord toward our families. It may seem that our obedience to the Lord will subject our loved ones to needless dangers, but this cannot be. The safest place in the entire world is the revealed will of God.

The disciples of our Lord Jesus were very concerned that He would be in physical danger by returning to Jerusalem where His enemies were lying in wait to stone Him. Jesus responded with these words (in John 11:9-10):

> Are there not twelve hours in the day? If anyone walks in the day,
> he does not stumble, because he sees the light of this world. But
> if anyone walks in the night, he stumbles, because the light is not
> in him.

He was saying what Solomon said in Proverbs 10:9: "He who walks in integrity walks securely." The path of duty is ever the path of safety. If God has called us to minister unto Him in a certain place and to take our family there, even to a dangerous environment, there is where we must be. A thousand times more dangerous is it to be in a comfortable place but out of His will.

Please do not read into these words a guarantee that your family will not fellowship with Jesus in His suffering. They surely will! But when that is the case, then the hardships are as sweet as they are redemptive.

My friend in the Lord, we cannot ever desire more for our families than the certainty that they are nestled in the center of the circle of the perfect will of God. How we would rob them if we tried to safeguard them from God's purposes!

Let us walk in the day. In the twelve hours of His revealed will there is security. We are sure to stumble if we skirt God's light in order to avoid temporal inconvenience and danger for the sake of our loved ones.

We do not have many choices to make. We have chosen the Lord, and as He unfolds His purposes for us, we have chosen His purposes as well. The safest place in the entire world is in the Master's will; the surest steps are taken in the light. If we are certain the light in us is indeed light and not darkness, then we may, by the undeserved promises of the New Covenant, walk in that light.

What a wonderful legacy to give to your children!

Be still and know the Lord.

6 In Him

*H*ave you ever thought you could make Bible verses come true if you believed hard enough? I identify so perfectly with the struggle and frustration you must have felt about the Christian experience. I remember especially trying to make Galatians 2:20 come true by my earnest faith. What a glorious rest the Lord brought into my heart when He showed my troubled soul that I was crucified with Christ whether I believed the fact or not.

My faith could neither quicken nor annul the fact. When my representative died on the cross, I died with Him. When He arose from the dead, with Him I also arose. In the eyes of God I am in Christ Jesus now, as He is seated at the right hand of the Majesty on high. When He returns, I will return with Him.

These facts are all true apart from my faith. My believing them cannot make them any more true than they are. Fact does not need faith to validate it. Believing something has no power to make it more or less true. Truth stands by itself, apart from faith.

I actually thought I had made progress in my life when I moved from trying to crucify myself by legalistic self-denials to attempting to make objective facts subjectively real by earnest faith.

Aren't you glad, believing friend, that neither unbelief nor faith can in any way change the everlasting facts of the gospel? By the finished work of our Lord Jesus, all the facts of the gospel are objectively true. He is dead to sin; He is alive to God; He has ascended to the Father's right hand; He has overcome the world; He has triumphed.

I am in Him who is dead to sin, alive to God, seated at the Father's right hand, has overcome the world and gloriously triumphed.

I cannot fly, but if I am in the airplane that is flying, I can be said to be flying. I am *in Him* who is dead to sin; therefore I am dead to sin! I am in Him who is alive unto God; therefore I am alive unto God! I have every reason to be of good cheer, not because I shall overcome the world, but because He has overcome the world and I am in Him. The apostle Paul rejoiced that he was always being led about in His triumph. We enter, by invitation, into His rest.

Only One has victory, and His name is Jesus. We have Him who has victory. For us who have Christ, victory is a person. We have union with Him, and we enjoy the spoils of His glorious and completed work.

We do long in our spirits to realize the fruit of His travail, but we would take great bounds forward if we would first recognize His accomplishments. If we recognize the facts that Jesus has made objectively true, in due time the Holy Spirit will make those facts subjectively real in our lives. We must recognize before we can realize.

Rather than trying to make something true by believing it, let us ask God to open our hearts to the glorious fullness of our union with the Lord Jesus. We are in Him who is wonderfully exalted, and we are heirs of all that belongs to Him. This is so even if we struggle to believe it.

A great burden will be lifted from your heart as God increasingly dawns on you the truth of your identification with the Savior. Faith may affect your peace, but it cannot touch your security.

God rest you!

WHEN I FACE TRIALS...

1 Eat the Scroll

*I*magine the situation the prophet Ezekiel found himself in (perhaps not so different from yours) when a scroll was handed to him from the Lord, written on both sides with bad news: lamentations, mournings, and woes. Then Ezekiel was given a strange command. He was told to eat the scroll.

The scroll did not, from all outward appearances, look very appetizing; there was nothing written on the heavenly menu that was pleasant to the flesh. It was a report that was all negative and gloomy. No matter which way Ezekiel turned the scroll, on the front and on the back, there were only bitter things written. "Eat the scroll" was thus an impossible command to obey apart from divine assistance. To swallow such a message was distasteful to the nth degree.

My own words here to you will not in any way change the purposes of God that have already been inscribed on the scroll given to you from heaven, but they may help you to imitate the faith of the dear prophet.

Ezekiel was enabled, by God's grace, to consume the bitter scroll. The Bible records (in Ezekiel 3:2) that God, by grace, fed it to him. Since it is as unnatural for us today, as it was for Ezekiel then, to embrace and devour a message so devastating, it is comforting to know that the Lord Himself will enable us to open our mouths and swallow His seemingly bitter truth.

It is not only Ezekiel who was naturally weak, but all the great men and women of God whose lives are recorded for us on the pages of the Scriptures. The Bible saints were as weak in themselves as we are.

Even after the scroll was in Ezekiel's mouth, he was reluctant to swallow it. "Feed your stomach and fill your body with this scroll which I am giving you," the Lord told him.

At last, by the grace of God, Ezekiel was enabled to swallow the scroll God had instructed him to eat, and when he swallowed it, the bitter scroll was transformed into the sweetest thing Ezekiel had ever eaten. God's will for Ezekiel became sweet as he appropriated it. That which was difficult to swallow at first became sweetness itself.

If difficult things are facing you in the days and weeks ahead, have no doubt that the Lord will be as faithful to you as He was to Ezekiel. Eating the scroll will honor the Lord who has ordained it for you. You will discover that there is sweetness in bringing honor to Him. Eating the scroll God has handed to you will crowd you more closely to Jesus, and the experience will conform you more to His likeness. No matter how bitter it seems to the flesh, there is sweetness in being more conformed to Jesus.

In addition to the sweetness you will personally experience in your spirit, eating the scroll will also be a testimony for all those who are watching you relate to the Lord. They are aware of the difficult thing that He has asked you to swallow. There is certainly sweetness in being used redemptively in the lives of others.

We should not fear the will of God. It is only to our mortality that the scroll seems bitter. God's purposes are as wise as they are loving, and His name and reputation are advanced as we consume the scroll that He hands down to us, whatever may be written on it. If you fear the things that have been decreed for you, you fear needlessly. Yield to Him. Eat the scroll, and in eating, may you discover the sweetness of His will as you acquiesce to His purposes for and through you!

2 Joy After Sorrow

*T*his may be a time when you are patiently enduring sorrow by the power of the life of God within you. Your testimony of God's sufficient grace will spread rapidly and bring great honor to God and encouragement to those who wonder how *they* would fare if called upon to suffer the same affliction.

Two Old Testament saints come now to mind. I think of Jacob's son Joseph and of Job. Both suffered redemptively; both suffered severely; both suffered for an extended period of time; and in both cases, the end of the long suffering brought God's great benediction.

One chief difference between the suffering of Job and that of Joseph is beautifully expressed in the words of the Lord Jesus: "Your sorrow shall be turned to joy" (John 16:20). In Job's case, joy followed sorrow; in Joseph's situation, sorrow was turned to joy.

There was little correspondence between the sufferings experienced by Job and the tenfold blessing he received after his long ordeal. His loss of children and property, the deterioration of his health and relationships, the disappointment of losing the honor of his testimony and the spiritual loyalty of his life's companion—these had little or nothing to do with the great blessings that followed. Any dissolving of the creature comforts that made up his hedge would have accomplished God's purpose in his life. God was testing Job's faith, and by the grace of God, Job came to see that the Lord Himself was all sufficient even when the hedge was down. God blessed Job after his fiery ordeal.

The suffering of Joseph, on the other hand, had great connection to the blessing that followed. The exaltation of Joseph as the bread of life for the whole world (a blessed foreshadowing of our Lord Jesus) depended upon the sufferings he endured in the years of his humiliation. His sufferings were the mother of his joy. Not only did joy follow Joseph's sufferings; his sufferings were actually turned into joy.

Without the jealousy of his brothers, Joseph would not have been sold as a slave. Without that slavery, he would not have come to Egypt. Without the lie Potiphar's wife told about him, he would not have been unjustly thrown into a prison where the word of the Lord could test him. Without being forgotten by those whose dreams he interpreted, he would not have been sought out to interpret Pharaoh's dreams. Without interpreting Pharaoh's dreams, he would never have been exalted. You see, every suffering was organically connected to the next in such a way that God's result and glorious end could be accomplished.

Everything Joseph endured was necessary to create the joy that would finally issue from his sorrow. Through his sorrows, salvation was brought to the world and repentance to his brothers. It was because his sorrow was turned into joy that he could say, "You meant evil against me but God meant it for good." When Joseph finally entered his joy, he could look back at his sorrow and praise God for it. He could see how the road of sorrow led him to the place of joy.

I do not know in your case if joy will follow sorrow or if your sorrow will be turned into joy. Either way, joy is the crowning end of your grief. Your fixed trust in Him and the settled rest you enjoy through it all will minister in a mighty way to all who have been observing God in your life. They will see that the whole issue is incidental to your faith.

May your sorrow soon come to an end and may unspeakable joy soon flood your spirit.

Rest!

3 Under God's Pruning Shears

*A*s you patiently bear by God's grace His severe dealings in your life, you may think of yourself as being under His "chastening rod." God's wisdom in His discipline is indeed something to rejoice in. But in this severity you may be experiencing a different ministry of the Father's heart. It is possible that you are not under His rod but under His pruning shears.

In the wonderful parable on abiding in the vine, our Lord Jesus told us that His Father is the Husbandman—the Vinedresser. He is the One whose work it is to prune the fruitful.

The variety of instruments He uses for pruning may feel exactly like the Father's rod of discipline, but the purpose of the pruning shears is very different. It is not the rebellious that He prunes. The backslider is chastened to teach him the importance of abiding in Christ; the fruitful are pruned because they are already abiding in Christ. It is not those who have gotten off track with the Lord and have been unfaithful that are pruned, but those who are abiding in the Lord Jesus and are bearing fruit. The Father prunes in order that their fruit will increase and remain.

Such a ministry is to be received from the hand of your heavenly Father. You have much reason to rejoice, because the lopping hook is in His wise hand and not in the hands of any group or individual. Untold damage has been done to God's dear people because of mis-pruning. There are proper times to be pruned and proper cuts to be made. Different results are attained by pruning when the sap flows than pruning when the plant is dormant. An elliptical cut produces one effect, a round cut another. Sometimes amputation is necessary for the survival of the fruit; at other times, just a heading back or a thinning out is all that is needed. Pruning may be done to the roots or to the limbs. For the mature vine it is done one way, for the sapling another.

Consider the possibility that the Lord is pruning you and not chastening you. The only practical difference it would make is that you would remove the sackcloth of mourning and put on the garments of praise. In both cases you would trust His grace to thankfully endure.

There is no fear in being cut back to the Vine!

4 Salvation from Sin's Consequences

*Y*ou may think at times that you have no claim on God's victory because you are suffering the consequences of your own sin and blunders. The gospel of Christ includes that possibility. But God has a song for us to sing even when we are reaping the tares that our own hands have foolishly sown.

When you have a season for quiet meditation, please ponder the wonder of the third Psalm. This is one of the psalms introduced to us with a historical heading. The heading before Psalm 3 is, "A psalm of David, when he fled from Absalom his son." David is fleeing from the consequences of his own sin. Absalom was born as the result of a polygamous relationship with Maacah, the princess of Geshur. If David had fully embraced the Lord's heart, this son would never have been born.

In the heat of vindictive rage, Absalom murdered his half brother Amnon for violating his natural sister, Tamar. It was because Absalom was David's son that the penalty for the crime of murder was never imposed, and Absalom escaped with his life. When Absalom later stole the hearts of the people and fostered an insurrection to murder his own father in order to usurp the throne, David fled into the wilderness.

Psalm 3 was written as the testimony of David at this time. Wouldn't you expect the psalm to be gloomy and melancholy? One would think that David would be saying, "I don't deserve Your deliverance, Lord! This is my own fault! Because of my polygamy and my failure to execute justice, this man now pursues my life. If it were a foreign enemy desiring my overthrow, I would expect Your intervention, but my present flight and fear for my life is because of the consequences of my own sin. I cannot expect victory! What right do I have to cry out for deliverance?"

But the exact opposite is true. David is not at all a victim of his past. He is not in bondage to the trouble that issued from his own blunders. Even when he was in trouble because of his own sin, he expected God to shield him and to lift up his discouraged head. He was able to have a peaceful sleep because he was convinced the Lord was sustaining him. It is marvelous to see how completely free from fear this lover of God was, even though he was running from the results of his own failures.

It is no wonder that when Jonah the prophet was suffering the consequences of his own sin, and the great deep engulfed him, he looked from his pit into heaven and began singing from David's psalm, "Salvation is of the Lord."

God's salvation is so wonderful it even includes deliverance from the enemies that our own failures may have created. Glorious grace!

Yes, my friend, there is always victory in the Lord. Absalom may bring great trouble into our lives, but he is not able to disturb our rest in the Lord. He cannot rob us of our victory. God delights to be our Glory and the Lifter of our heads. He will turn the curse into a blessing.

Pull out all the stops and sing David's psalm with all your heart! We are never at the mercy of our enemies, even if the enemy is the harvest of our own sowing.

5 He Heals the Brokenhearted

A physician may bind a fractured or broken bone, but how can a man mend a broken heart? I will not pretend to always understand or identify with such suffering by another; I only desire to point such a one to Him who is said to be able to heal the brokenhearted and to bind up their wounds. How He will accomplish this cure for the brokenhearted, I am not prepared to predict. But I am certain He will!

Directly after we read in Psalm 147 of how God heals the brokenhearted and binds up their wounds, we see this proclamation: "He counts the number of the stars; He gives names to all of them. Great is our Lord and abundant in strength. His understanding is infinite."

God invites the brokenhearted person to gaze into the starry heavens and consider His abundant power and infinite wisdom. Perhaps this is because the brokenhearted saint feels like a vacant star overwhelmed and lost in the vastness of endless space. God desires the hurting heart to consider how stars, light-years apart and galaxies away, are all numbered and named by Him. It must minister great comfort to those who feel enveloped in a multitude of beings to know that God gives individual attention to every star in the heavens.

The aching heart of His redeemed child cannot go unnoticed by Him who is so attentive to a universe of lifeless matter. O friend, lift up your head and observe the works of His fingers. This power and wisdom, by which God oversees the universe, He desires to apply to your broken heart.

You may imagine your own wound to be incurable. I counsel you in the love of the Lord to meditate on Psalm 147:3-5. See that the Holy Spirit has joined together the healing of broken hearts and the governing of the starry host. The Lord wants you to know that He is willing to apply His infinite wisdom and power to your case. He can fix your bleeding heart.

6 Life's Changing Scenes

*P*aul says in 1 Corinthians 7 that "the time has been shortened" and that "the form of this world is passing away."

Those who are acquainted with the Greek language tell us that the apostle's references here were borrowed from the acting stage. He used expressions that describe the changing scenes of a drama as the curtain rises and falls on the successive acts of the play. "The form [or fashion] of this world is passing away," he reminds us. In the same way that act one vanishes to make room for act two and act two for act three, so the "time is narrowed," he says. The time for each act is predetermined and short; soon the curtain will fall on that scene and rise on another.

In a play the scenes may change suddenly and dramatically. We may be observing a happy occasion—a marriage, a graduation, a picnic, the birth of a baby, or a promotion—when the curtain suddenly falls. When it rises again, we may hear the doleful notes of the funeral dirge or behold some devastation or injustice. The curtain rises and falls many times during the course of the performance, carrying the audience through the wide range of changing and powerful emotions.

Paul, it appears, was warning the Christians in Corinth of the possibilities of becoming consumed by the power of the play. When the curtain rose on scenes of sorrow, they were profoundly consumed by sorrow; when the curtain rose on scenes of celebration, they were carried away with uncontrolled exuberance. Paul was not suggesting that the believers become detached and stoical when the scenes of life changed, but he was reminding them of the true source of their joy and contentment. The curtain will be rising and falling over and over again on the stage of life. Sometimes it will rise on strength, joy, and prosperity; other times it will rise on weakness, sadness, and affliction.

We must not be consumed in any way by these fleeting scenes. We must ever focus upon Christ, the Source of all true joy and contentment. We must never confuse the expressions of joy and contentment with the Source of true joy and contentment.

Relating to a life partner or a loving family, for example, is a wonderful expression of our joy in the Lord, but it must not become the source. As wonderful as marriage and family are, they are not the true source of joy or contentment. Only the Lord Jesus is such a source. Just so, Christian fellowship is a wonderful expression of joy and contentment, but not the source. Only Christ is the Source.

Any success or material possession or season of relaxation can express our joy and rest, but it can never be the source of that contentment. When the curtain rises on prosperity for us, as inevitably it will, we must keep our eyes upon Christ. When the curtain rises on some disappointment or loss for us, as inevitably it will, we must keep our eyes upon Jesus. He is the Source of our joy and contentment.

We may laugh and weep, rejoice and grieve, but any changing scene of our fleeting life must never master us. Only the Lord is essential; nonessentials come and go and we should not be too much moved by their arrival or departure.

Christ is our substance. We must refuse to be controlled by the unsubstantial things in life. The Christian must ever take Christ seriously, but we must learn not to take life too seriously. Only Christ can keep us content when we abound and when we suffer loss. May we learn the contentment Paul learned through Christ who strengthened him.

7 Our Faithful Creator

*T*he manifestation of the Lord Jesus is unpredictable. While we expect to behold Him as High Priest or Sympathetic Father, He may manifest Himself in some other way that will perfectly meet our deepest need.

You may want to enjoy Christ now as your intimate Friend. But His ways are not our ways. The way we think we need to behold Him may not be the manifestation of Christ that will best suit our present need.

The apostle Peter instructed those who suffered according to the will of God to commit their souls "to a faithful Creator." Why do you suppose that those who were enduring undeserved suffering would need a manifestation of the Lord as a faithful Creator? Wouldn't you think they would need to appropriate the Lord as the God of all comfort or a loving parent? Yet the Holy Spirit, through the apostle Peter, invites the suffering Christian to surrender to the Lord as unto a faithful Creator.

Perhaps it is because when we are going through the experience of rejection by those who are close to us, we do not have naturally what it takes to endure. What a joy to know that when we do not have what it takes, we have Him who can *create* what it takes to patiently endure. We always have a faithful Creator living in our hearts!

The Lord will reveal Himself to you in the way He knows will best meet your need. He may show Himself as your dearest friend, as you desire; He may show Himself in some other way. I am sure He will meet your earnest desire to see Him with a suitable manifestation of Himself to your heart. An infinite God will have no problem meeting you exactly as you need to behold Him. He will visit you with a transforming vision of Himself. We dare not dictate the time or manner of His appearing, but let us rest expectantly in the fact of it. Meditate day and night in His word and be open and ready to appropriate Him as the Holy Spirit proposes Him to you.

These shadows will soon flee away. Wait patiently for Him!

8 Look Beyond Faith

You must not blame your weak faith for any present difficult circumstances. You probably think that if your faith were stronger or greater or more sincere, you would experience the deliverance you so passionately desire. That is not necessarily the case. Sometimes deliverance from troubles is part of God's redemptive purposes. However, deliverance in the midst of adverse circumstances is always God's redemptive purpose. It is possible to have joy and contentment in your spirit while you walk with the Son of God in your fiery furnace.

It is true that over and over again, by faith, the Old Testament saints trusted God to work miracles for them just as we see in Hebrews 11. They "conquered kingdoms...shut the mouths of lions, quenched the power of fire, escaped the edge of the sword, from weakness were made strong, became mighty in war, put foreign enemies to flight. Women received back their dead by resurrection"—all of these wonders were attributed to faith. It is no marvel, after contemplating these things that were written for our instruction, that we would expect to see the same kind of response from the Lord to our own humble faith.

But the end of the same chapter tells a different story. There is another aspect to the same quality of faith. We read that by faith "some were tortured, others experienced mockings and scourgings, some were dragged away in chains and thrown into dungeons." By faith, the saints "were stoned, sawn in two, murdered by the sword;

they went about in sheepskins and goatskins, they were often desti-
tute, afflicted, and ill treated." If they had faith, why weren't they
delivered? Was their faith to blame? Why do we read that by faith
they wandered "in deserts and mountains and caves and holes in the
ground"? Wouldn't you think if they had enough faith, God would
have delivered them?

It is very important to realize that some, by faith, are delivered;
some, by the same excellent faith, are not delivered. Deliverance has
little to do with faith.

Perhaps the safest thing for us to do is to take our eyes off faith
altogether and fix them on Jesus. The important thing after all about
faith is the dear Lord Jesus, the grand object of true faith.

We know He will not share His glory with another. Certainly He
will not share His glory with something called faith. It is He who
delivers, not faith! Faith is great when it lays hold of the infinite Savior. Faith depends upon Him. He delivers or does not deliver, as best
serves our highest interests and His greatest glory.

Let us both read again the wonderful eleventh chapter of Hebrews and discover God's heart on the nature of faith. Then let us
read on to Hebrews 12:2 and fix our eyes on Jesus, the author and
perfecter of faith. So shall we find our rest. Knowing Him is better
than deliverance any day.

9 The Blessedness of Faith Without Sight

*S*ince all of our Lord's disciples struggled at times with their faith, why did the Holy Spirit single out Thomas in John 20 to represent all unbelieving believers? We do not speak about "doubting Philip" or "doubting Peter" or "doubting James." What is Thomas's contribution to the history of redemption? There must be a reason.

It may be that Thomas failed more in his privilege than in his faith. Thomas was singled out of all the disciples to represent the entire church age. He stood in the very shoes of every believer who would follow him. Thomas was given the privilege to believe in the risen Savior on the very same basis and grounds that we are called upon to believe in Him.

Thomas had the testimony of Scripture, as we have. In the same way we are called upon to believe reliable witnesses, he was called upon to believe the testimony of reliable witnesses who had been convinced by infallible proofs from God that Jesus was alive. It would appear that the Lord desired to illustrate through Thomas the blessedness of believing without seeing. When Thomas insisted on sight before he would believe, he lost the superlative privilege of leading the church into the highest means of knowing God.

It is almost certain that the Lord will not appear physically to us in a room where the doors are shut, as He did to the early disciples.

He most probably will not invite us to literally touch His glory wounds with our hands, nor will we actually see or speak with angels at His empty tomb. Those infallible signs were granted to the early witnesses.

Thomas was selected to represent us. He was as we are. He was chosen to teach us how to appropriate the living Christ by the simplicity of faith without the subjective evidence of sight. He was not denied (at first) the experience of beholding the living Savior because he had less faith than the ten who saw Him, but rather because he was selected by the Lord to display to the church of all ages the blessedness that issues from faith without sight.

Although Thomas did not live up to the high privilege he was offered because of unbelief, nevertheless, by the reversing grace of God, he did not miss the revelation of the Savior. The Lord Jesus condescended to Thomas's cry for empirical evidence. Thomas became another eyewitness of the resurrected Christ.

As the Lord was patient with Thomas and revealed Himself in spite of this man's struggling faith, so He will ever manifest Himself to us, even if we wrestle with the same doubts that plagued Thomas.

Beyond all doubt, there is a more excellent way!

If it is true that Thomas stood that day where we stand today, then it is also true that we stand today where Thomas stood on that first Easter. We must not wonder or resist if the Lord increasingly denies us the subjective sense of His presence. We have the same privilege Thomas was offered. We may become object lessons of the blessedness that comes from believing without sight. We do not need to see Him with our physical eyes or touch Him with our physical hands. We have the Scriptures; we have the testimony of reliable witnesses!

May God grace us so that we will not give in to our flesh and insist on sight. If we are content in Christ by simple faith apart from sight, that simple faith will have a powerful influence in the hearts of all that follow after us.

The world knows nothing of the blessedness that comes by faith apart from sight. Sadly, the church knows little about such blessedness. May that blessedness become ours to enjoy and share.

10   The Miracle of Patience

*H*ave you prayed for patience? It's only by the Lord's power that the patience you seek can be expressed in your life. Patience is a grace of God and a characteristic of the love that is the fruit of His Spirit. For patience to have its perfect work in any believer, a mighty miracle of God is required.

The apostle Paul prayed that the Colossian believers would be "strengthened with all power, according to His glorious might, for *the attaining of all steadfastness and patience*" (Colossians 1:11). Is it possible that the glorious omnipotence of God is required to enable a Christian to be patient under trials? Indeed! Apart from God's miracle there can be no patience. How many times must we fail before we realize that patience is not in us?

Unless God has mercy on us and grants us patience, we shall remain impatient all of our days. To be thankfully indifferent to worldly comforts and enjoyments is absolutely unnatural.

Patience abounds in Him in infinite fullness. Patience, far from being a gift He grants to us apart from Christ, is experienced through our union with Him. God does not give us the Lord Jesus and a virtue called patience. He only gives us His Son. If we have Him, we have patience. The more we are conformed to His likeness, like Him, we will cheerfully submit unto the Lord in all things. Knowing that His dominion is over all things concerning us enables us to rest patiently upon Him.

May God grant you the patience you desire by increasing your heart's vision of the Lord Jesus. The kingdom is God's. The power is God's. The glory is God's. The blessing belongs to us forever.

May God strengthen you with all power according to His glorious might for the attaining of all steadfastness and patience.

Rest!

11 The Test of Praise

*H*ow will God test our faith?

Perhaps the answer to that question is swallowed up in a larger question: What does the Lord mean when He speaks in Scripture of the test of faith? More precious than gold, which perishes, the Lord reminds us, is the testing of our faith.

What constitutes a test of faith and why is it so precious in the Lord's eyes?

Faith, in its simplest form, is trusting Jesus. The test of faith, in its simplest form, is the opportunity to trust Jesus. God deems the opportunity to trust in Him more precious than gold. You can see how unlimited the applications of this truth would be. The Lord is continually orchestrating our circumstances that we might have and apply opportunities to trust Him.

No Christian is without the testing of faith. Every day God provides fresh opportunities to trust Jesus. The testing may come from above, beneath, within, or all around. Usually we think of the testing of our faith in terms of the common trials of life. Distractions, to be sure, are a great opportunity for us to trust the Lord. Physical or mental affliction provides an occasion to trust Him. Faith is tested in our relationships with other people. Personal limitations provide hourly occasions to **depend** upon the Lord. In whatever direction we look, we can find opportunities to turn the eyes of our faith toward Him. Precious opportunities to look to Jesus, like the poor, will always be with us.

It is difficult to gauge one test over another, since many things drive us to Jesus in different ways, but wise Solomon tells of one test of faith that seems to surpass many others. Although it is one of our greatest opportunities to trust the Lord, yet for many the opportunity has been wasted because of pride. We see the test mentioned in Proverbs 27:21:

The crucible is for silver and the furnace for gold,
And each is *tested by the praise accorded him.*

No threat to the physical body, no dissolving of creature comforts, no dissipation of hope, no undeserved treatment from our enemies, no amount of isolation will test the reality of our faith in Jesus like a compliment blown our way. The slightest expression of admiration, the smallest hint of approbation, the most insignificant step of exaltation is indeed a furnace to test our faith. The flesh lusts after credit and honor and will rarely recognize the need to trust the Lord. Our natural hearts are so full of pride and self-conceit that we become strangers to ourselves and easily forget that we live and stand by the free grace of God. The Builder of the house receives glory, not the house; the Defender of the city must receive the praise.

We are more apt to trust Jesus when we take a blow on the cheek than when we receive a pat on the back. The praise of men to men is a severe test of our faith.

Even in this furnace, however, we may be delighted by the presence of the Lord and preserved from harm, as were the three Hebrews in the days of Nebuchadnezzar when they walked with Him in their furnace.

We will all be tested daily by fresh opportunities to trust Jesus. The need to manifest Jesus to the world demands it; our need to be conformed to Him requires it. Every test is designed to cultivate an intimate fellowship with the Lord.

He graces His slaughtered flock to rejoice on the martyr's block. May He also grace us when we are tested by the praise of men.

How vain we must be in ourselves to be vulnerable to such a feather! Buy up every opportunity!

12 His Soundproof Pavilion

I have discovered a passage from the Bible that will completely extinguish the flame with which others try to incinerate your peace with the Lord.

When the words of those who misrepresent you swarm around your ears like bees, and lying witnesses are attempting to sting you with falsehoods, there is a place of silence and safety from the strife of tongues. David sang about the soundproof pavilion in Psalm 31:20. It was called the secret place of God's presence:

> In the covert of thy presence wilt thou hide them from the
> plottings of man:
> Thou wilt keep them secretly in a pavilion from the strife of
> tongues. (ASV)

Run swiftly to the Lord Himself and abide in His presence. There you will be safe and out of earshot from the accusations that are being hurled at you. In His presence there is fullness of joy. In the soundproof pavilion of His company, you will dwell beyond the reach of all the arrows designed for your destruction. There you will be secretly nourished and your soul will thrive; the malicious intentions of the enemy will be utterly frustrated. You will emerge from the secret place as the three Hebrew children emerged from Nebuchadnezzar's furnace. Not one hair of your head will be singed, nor will the smell of smoke be upon you. You will come forth both radiant and free.

There is no other security from the strife of tongues. Only in His presence will you be safeguarded against the spirit of vindication and animosity, which are nature's response to the smiting of the cheek.

You are in no danger from the strife of tongues. A Christian is never at the mercy of any person or circumstance. God's providence rules and overrules all that touches us. The only snare we really need to fear comes from within. Our response to the injustice directed against us is the only spiritual threat from which we must flee.

Let us run to Jesus! He will make us blind and deaf to the weapons framed against us. Let them tire themselves out with words of vanity while we enjoy sweet fellowship with Jesus.

May you discover and enter the soundproof pavilion of the presence of the Lord.

13 More Than the Sands

*D*o the number and intensity of your troubles seem only to grow?

If I was able, and I am not, I would point you to promises from God's Word that specifically answer each trial you are facing. If I were with you, I believe we could gather a wonderful collection of relevant promises equaling at least five times the number of the things that are weighing you down. Perhaps others who are better acquainted with the Scriptures might be able to suggest seven or ten words of appropriate consolation to apply to each anxiety and hurt you experience. A roomful of godly counselors may be able to discover twenty or thirty applicable promises for each pressure that is upon you. I suppose that if the reality were known, the suitable promises would outnumber your problems by many thousands.

David, in a poetical fountain of praise, wrote Psalm 139:17-18:

How precious also are Your thoughts to me, O God!…
If I should count them, they would outnumber the sand.

Outnumber the sand! How long would it take for modern technology to count the grains of sand that could fill even a teacup? How many grains of sand would it require to fill a child's small pail? Beyond all calculation would be the number of grains of sand on a single beach. How many beaches rim the waters of the world? How many deserts of sand stretch for many hundreds of miles? Is it possible that God actually thinks about you more than the number of the grains of sands that are upon the earth? If He thinks of you more than this, I ask, "How much more?" Does the Lord think of you ten times more than this countless number? Is it twenty times more? Does God think of you a million times more?

He is the almighty God! He is infinite! Psalm 139:17-18 is more than a poetical hyperbole in the mouth of a worshiping psalmist. Infinitely more than the number of the grains of sand upon the earth is the number of the Lord's thoughts toward you.

Adverse circumstances may seem to be swarming against you in overwhelming numbers, but consider the astounding number of thoughts God has daily toward you. The staggering figure would humble any thoughtful child of God to the dust.

Add to that awesome fact the further truth that every single thought God has toward you is a *precious* thought. Oh, if we only knew His heart, His mind, His wonderful purposes for us! If we knew, we would bless Him without intermission for all He has engineered and allowed in our lives.

Allow this passage in the Psalms to pillow your troubled head. I am sure that your inner person, after meditating on the precious and vast thoughts of the Lord toward you in Christ Jesus, will be renewed. You will count your affliction light and momentary, producing for you an eternal weight of glory far beyond the weak comparisons of the numbers of grains of sand on this planet.

Focus on things eternal.

Rest! Worship!

14 The Dread of Broken Fellowship with God

*I*n the days of His flesh," we read of our Savior in Hebrews 5:7, "He offered up both prayers and supplications with loud crying and tears to the One able to save Him from death, and He was heard because of His piety." When did Jesus do this? In Gethsemane? On Calvary? What an amazing mystery!

Perhaps it was in Gethsemane that our Lord Jesus was becoming sin for us. It would be difficult to explain His agony there, which could wring blood from His pores, without seeing His suffering in the background of severe spiritual warfare.

Clearly there was more going on in Gethsemane than the devoutest hearts have yet discovered. We know the servant is not above his master, yet we have heard of the testimonies of His martyred saints who appear to have died more bravely (I speak as a fool) than our Lord Jesus. It cannot be! When our Lord Jesus recoiled from the cup in Gethsemane, He was not shrinking from suffering or death. No! He was dreading the experience of broken fellowship with His holy Father, God. There was never a time before, in all of the long ages of eternity, when Jesus was separated from God. This was to be a new experience for God. He knew that the cup represented the separation from God that sin deserved. Oh, how His holy soul must have trembled at the thought of being forsaken by God!

This is what we should shrink from as well. To be cut off from fellowship with God should be repulsive to our very being. We must not faint in the face of pain or death, but we must ever cower in horror at the possibility of severing fellowship with Him.

Thankful we are that our Lord Jesus drained that cup to its dregs! It was filled, the psalmist reminds us, with snares, fire and brimstone, and burning wind. How different is the cup we are called upon to drink! He is the portion of our cup, which runs over on all sides at all times.

O Lord! Help us shrink back in holy dread from the sin that would separate us from a moment's fellowship with You.

15 We Must Not Misread the Works of the Lord

*H*ow many strangers has God sent our way who turned out to be ministering angels? How many ravens have flown into our lives, bearing the provision of the Lord? How many messengers from Satan have actually hand-delivered to us the message of the Lord?

We must not make evil interpretations of the mercies God showers upon us. We must be careful not to misread His works and imagine that His blessing is actually a curse.

You may have interpreted recent difficulties as a sign of God's displeasure with you. Perhaps you have run to the saints with a downcast spirit and have spelled out a long litany of reasons why the Lord might have reasons to afflict you. I wish every believer were as sensitive toward the Lord as that—swift to humble themselves under His mighty hand. I would not discourage that spirit.

However, your severity with yourself may be clouding your eyes from seeing a wonderful benediction from the Lord. Not all affliction is the result of the Father's rod of discipline. Some trials, like the sufferings of the apostle Paul, are designed to be redemptive.

Do you remember the story of Mary Magdalene? She loved the Lord Jesus as you love the Lord. She could not bear to be a moment out of His favor. In her haste to minister unto Him, she misread a great symbol of the gospel. She saw from a distance the huge stone that was before the Savior's grave, and it was rolled away. This was intended to communicate good news. It was the symbol of glorious tidings; it was the sign of victory. The stone rolled away told the story of a risen Savior.

Mary, however, took the moved stone to be an evidence of bad news. To her it related the story of a rifled grave and a stolen savior. Because she misread the mighty work of God, she brought great sorrow to her own heart.

All students of the Bible have been profoundly moved at the story of Mary, standing with a flood of tears streaming down her face in the very presence of the Savior she deeply loved, and yet missing Him completely because she misread His works. She actually took Jesus to be the gardener and accused Him of being her enemy. She blamed Jesus for stealing the body of Jesus! Oh, how much she lost because she did not see God's heart in His works!

No one else can fully know God's mysterious providence in your life by His allowing your present trials. Yet I ask you to be sensitive and alert to the possibility that there is good news inherent in your affliction. You must not misread His work in your life. What you are facing is perfectly consistent with His infinite love and wisdom. It is like the stone that was rolled away from the tomb. It is the opportunity for you to experience a living savior. Do not read an ill message into that which God is intending to be a benediction to you and to all who touch your life.

The Lord is not robbing you of the presence of the Lord. He is not the gardener. Ask the Lord to show Himself, and the day will soon come when you will bless His name for the honey in your hive.

May the Lord call your name and hug your spirit as He did to sister Mary Magdalene.

WHEN I WRESTLE
WITH QUESTIONS...

1 We Are Like the Wind

*H*ave you ever been troubled in your spirit because you could not identify the day and the hour when you first claimed a saving interest in Christ? So many testify so clearly of the very day of their salvation, and some demand such a testimony from others, as if it were an indispensable evidence of true faith in the Savior. Those who are not able to identify the specific moment of their spiritual birth are often made to feel insecure. The unsettled question robs them of assurance and peace.

I wonder if this disturbance of rest is not another of the enemy's many subtle underminings of faith in an attempt to place the true child of God under condemnation.

When our Lord Jesus was instructing Nicodemus (in John 3) about the necessity of the new birth, He used the wind as an illustration. His point was that the Holy Spirit, like the wind, does an invisible work in His comings and goings.

We cannot answer every question about the wind, but we cannot deny its existence. We can hear the sound of it as it whistles through the trees; we can see its effects by the moving of those things in its path. I call attention to this because it illustrates a wonderful truth.

It is not really the person of the Holy Spirit who is being pictured by the wind, but the work of the Holy Spirit. After Jesus called attention to the mysteries of the wind, He said, "so is everyone who is born of the Spirit."

The wind is not primarily an illustration of the Spirit of God; it is a picture of those who are born of the Spirit. The wind is a picture of the Christian. Ah, what a wonderful truth to send relief to the heart that is troubled about identifying the starting point of spiritual life with the Lord. Jesus said that those who are born of the Spirit, like the wind, could not accurately pinpoint when their life in Christ began. The new birth, like the wind, is known by its visible effects, but there is much mystery as to when it started or where it is going. We must leave those secrets with the Lord.

I would not be surprised, when all things are fully known, if those who supposed their spiritual life began on a certain date and time were mistaken.

The time a life is first conceived in a womb is different from the time a baby is born. There is life before birth. Some may know fairly accurately when they were spiritually born, but who can tell when God first implanted His Spirit into their hearts and they began to live?

To add to the mystery, remember that we were chosen in Him before the foundation of the world. Who would dare attempt to place a date on that?

Do not be tempted to look back for a particular experience that marked the beginning of your life in the Lord. We do not live by sight, but by faith. Jesus told us to rejoice not that we know when our names were inscribed in the Lamb's Book of Life, but that they are indeed written there.

Your assurance, and mine, comes from what is written. Let us rest in it!

2 Stronger Than the Strong Man

*T*he final chapter is not yet written. We must not conclude that Satan has won the war because he seems to have gained an upper hand in a conflict that amounts to a skirmish.

The Lord has not finished His glorious redemption. Although our enemy, the "strong man" (Luke 11:21), is fully armed and does seem to hold fast what he considers his own possessions, a stronger than the strong has manifested Himself. Jesus will bind the strong man, and his goods will be spoiled and distributed.

When we focus on ourselves, oh, how weak we appear! When we focus on the enemy, oh, how strong he appears! Fear fills our hearts. Let us focus on the Lord. Oh, how comforting! Joy floods our souls! By the finger of God He can disarm the strong man. By the breath of His mouth, He can destroy the Antichrist. By His mere appearing, He will put an end to all wrong.

When ancient Israel looked at themselves, they appeared to be but grasshoppers, while the enemy towered before them as giants. When they looked to the Lord, the Canaanites became as insignificant as grasshoppers.

Let us lift up our eyes to the Lord. By the power of God, those beloved ones who seem defeated will yet rise from the ashes to bless the Lord. We must not believe that they are down for the count. The work of the Lord goes on. Satan may have cast them down in violence, but they will rise to their feet without being harmed. Perhaps they will be hurt, but they will suffer no harm.

May God begin even now to wipe away the tears from their eyes and from yours.

We must be patient until God has finished His symphony. In that day we will marvel at what He has accomplished.

May God give you peace and rest in your spirit as you trust Him who is Victory.

God will shortly crush Satan under your feet.

3 Coming into the World, Jesus Speaks

*T*here is always mystery when we try to understand the two natures of our Lord Jesus Christ. We know that Jesus, as God, knows all things by omniscience and that, as a man, He increased in wisdom and stature and in favor with God and man, as Luke informs us. Jesus once declared that, as a man, He did not know the hour of His own return. Puzzling!

Some believe that a consciousness of Messiahship dawned only gradually on the humanity of Jesus. Some think that He discovered, by study and degrees, who He really was and what His mission included. I have heard some teach that Jesus began wondering if He was the Promised Seed at age twelve, and that He didn't finally realize it until His baptism by John.

I strongly believe that He knew from the very beginning, as God and man, who He was and what He had come to do.

There is a curious passage on the infancy of our Lord Jesus written in Hebrews 10. It begins with the words, "When He comes into the world, He says…"

This expression "when He comes into the world" undoubtedly refers to our Lord Jesus' incarnation. And what did He say on this occasion when He entered the world as a little infant? The verse continues:

Sacrifice and offering Thou hast not desired,
But a body Thou hast prepared for Me;
In whole burnt offerings and sacrifices for sin
    Thou has taken no pleasure.
Then I said, "Behold, I have come
(In the scroll of the book it is written of Me)
To do Thy will, O God."

I am quite sure these words were not spoken audibly that glorious night in Bethlehem. I cannot imagine that the ears of His mother, Mary, or His stepfather, Joseph, heard them. I do not think these words were heard by any of the shepherds who gathered around His crib. Nevertheless, He spoke them.

He spoke of the body that God had prepared for Him in which He would offer Himself as the true sacrifice for sin. He proclaimed from the manger, in fulfillment of all Bible prophecy, "I have come to do Thy will, O God." I would think that this is a reference to His humanity. I do not understand how a baby can know these things and articulate them, but I think the record is clear.

If I am correct, then Jesus knew from the earliest moment that He was the Messiah. He did not have to discover His identity or mission by studying the ancient writings or by special revelation of God to His spirit. He always knew who He was and why He came.

How, by pondering these mysteries, we are ever driven to the Lord Himself! In the final analysis the question is not, "When did Jesus come to know He was the true Messiah?" but, "When, by the undeserved grace of God, do *we* come to know that Jesus is the true Messiah?"

4 Veiling the Lesser Glory

*M*oses, who lived at the time of the Old Covenant but under the power and life of the new and everlasting covenant of God's grace, deliberately veiled the fading glory of the law from the view of God's people. He knew this glory was only skin-deep and temporary, and so that the sons of Israel would not focus on the lesser glory, he covered it up.

Sometimes it may be right to deliberately veil the glory of what may be called "the important things" in the church, so that God's people will not chase after any glory outside of the Lord Jesus Christ.

The study of missions is glorious, but not apart from the person of the Lord Jesus. There is a fading glory in the observations made by human wisdom concerning the family, interrelationships, character disciplines, or the proper functioning of a Christian community. Those things may seem important, but they are not Christ.

Beholding Christ in reality is the only way to learn His heart concerning the family. One will never discover how to relate to the greater family of God, or those outside the fold, by studying relationships. We must see Jesus! The fruit of beholding Him alone will sanctify and create within a missionary heart. We do not need to focus on the fading glory of spiritual gifts. Rather we need to embrace the full Savior, and any gift or gifts He bestows upon us will be intuitively exercised to the edification of the saints.

Being Christ-centered does not neglect the practical side of life. It guarantees it.

I highly esteem any minister of the New Covenant who not only presents the grace of God as the only rule of life, but who also has the moral courage to place a thick veil over all the good things that are not Christ.

Almost every believer will cheer when someone says, "Look to Jesus," because they do not really comprehend what is involved in that New Covenant invitation. How quickly the affirmations cease when the negative is added to clarify what it really means to look unto Jesus. Look to Jesus, not missions. Look to Jesus, not surrender or faith. Look to Jesus, not the precious ordinances. Look to Jesus, not Christian fellowship or discipleship or anything else.

The faithful minister of the New Covenant will not only invite the heart to embrace a solitary savior, but he will also encourage the heart to turn far away from pursuing all that is not Him.

Balance comes not by centering on issues, but by "holding fast to the head, from whom the entire body, being supplied and held together by the joints and ligaments, grows with a growth which is from God" (Colossians 2:19). This is how the Christian develops in a healthy way. The other "important things" will then burst forth as the sweet and precious fruit borne out of union with Jesus.

5 He Has Much More
to Give You Than This

*A*re you reeling from the devastating results of an impulsive or an unwise investment? Good king Amaziah received a word from the Lord (in 2 Chronicles 25) that may suit your situation.

Amaziah, without seeking the counsel of the Lord, hired one hundred thousand valiant mercenaries from Israel to join with his army of three hundred thousand men. For their service he paid, in advance, one hundred talents of silver (scholars estimate the value at fifty dollars for each soldier). Before this combined army went to battle against God's enemy, a man of God rebuked Amaziah for hiring the mercenaries and told him it was the Lord's pleasure that they not be used in the upcoming battle. If Amaziah continued with his plans, the man of God said, God would bring them down in defeat before the enemy.

The first question on the mind of Amaziah was, "What about the hundred talents of silver I've already paid out?" The thought of losing the money was a shock. What was he to do? What recourse did he have?

In response to Amaziah's concern, the word of the Lord was this: "The LORD has much more to give you than this." In other words, "Let it go! You made a terrible mistake when you acted without consulting the Lord. You have forfeited a great deal of money, but the Lord has much more to give you than this!"

It is God's pleasure for you to focus on Him. If there is a loss for you because of a presumptuous investment that must now be abandoned, it cannot be compared to the spiritual gain the Lord has for you if you trust Him. Amaziah was told to take his eyes off the loss and put them on the gain. The Lord did not forsake him just because he made a costly decision without God's blessing. Amaziah had to regard this loss as a part of the "all things" that would work together to help conform him to Christ.

I know it may seem overwhelming to you at the moment to realize that you may not be able to recover the money you have spent on "mercenaries," but believe the truth of God which promises that the Lord has much more to give you than this. Even at this time, you may go forward in uninterrupted fellowship with the Lord by drawing near to Him.

The Lord may have mercy on you and surprise you with some return. Be willing to let go of the rest. Focus on the Lord and the gain that will come from Him as true riches.

How rich God will make you with wealth that cannot be lost! He has much more to give you than anything you could lose of this world's coinage.

6 Sin Leading to Death

*T*hrough the years God's earnest servants have grappled with what was the intention of God's heart concerning His promise to give life, when we pray, to those who have committed "a sin not leading to death" (1 John 5:16). The confusion is magnified by His stated desire that we *not* pray for someone who has committed "a sin leading to death." Though we may desire not to be judgmental toward those who sin, yet here it is implied that we can and should discern the sin that leads to death. We should know when someone is guilty of that sin.

Although I cannot speak with absolute certainty about this strong language with which John ends his first epistle, yet I believe it is helpful to understand his comments by relating the conclusion of his letter to the introduction. In the opening chapter of this wonderful epistle on intimate fellowship with the Savior, the apostle John describes two kinds of Christians. There are those who walk imperfectly in light, and there are those who walk in darkness.

Those who walk imperfectly in light are those who are basically open to the Lord, and although they are not perfect, because these Christians desire to honor the Lord, the blood of the Lord Jesus is constantly cleansing them.

On the other hand, those who walk in darkness are those who have willfully rebelled against the Lord and His light, and by that rebellion are said to be in darkness. Those who are in darkness by willful sin are promised a just and thorough forgiveness only if they come to the Lord confessing their sin and failure. Our perfect Advocate in heaven is always ready to be the propitiation for our sins.

To be spiritually logical, it appears that Christians who walk imperfectly in light are the ones who have committed a sin not leading to death. They are the ones who are open to the Lord Jesus, even though there may be many areas of their lives in which they are not yet conformed to His likeness.

A Christian with a greater measure of light and maturity might find much that falls short of the full glory of God in one who is walking imperfectly in light. Although that imperfection is still called sin, it does not break the Christian's fellowship with the Lord because it is not willful. The precious blood of Jesus continually cleanses those who "walk in the Light as He Himself is in the Light." For these we must pray, and because they are open to the Savior, God has promised to grant them life in answer to our prayers.

It is a different case for those who willfully depart from the revealed will of God and choose to walk in darkness. They may be like those referred to by Paul in his first epistle to the Corinthians. They are weak or sickly or, in some cases, actually removed from this life by death, because of their refusal to walk with God in light.

For those who boldly and deliberately resist the Lord and, without shame or regret, choose darkness by rebelling against the Lord, it seems spiritually logical that they are beyond the help of our prayers. They must pray themselves. They must repent. They must come to the Lord, confessing their sin. They must, by confession, return to the light where the blood of Jesus can continually keep them clean. They can, by faith, apply themselves to the Savior. He is ever willing to forgive. It is the lifestyle that leads to death that militates against God's determination to give life to the unwilling. They are unwilling, and therefore we are commanded not to pray for them.

We have a great privilege to bring life to those who choose to walk in fellowship with God by praying for them. We cannot keep from grieving over those who walk in darkness, but our real prayer ministry is for those who walk imperfectly in light. Let us pray earnestly for one another!

May God keep us from choosing the path that breaks our fellowship with Him and leaves us in the dark world that even the prayers of the saints cannot penetrate.

7 The Lord's Remembrancers

I believe that every earnest thinking child of God has asked, "Will my prayer change the will of God? And if it will not, then what is the gain of prayer?" If God has already determined His purpose, what good will it do if prayer rises up to Him?

Certainly our prayers cannot change the will of God, but they can *fulfill* the will of the Lord. God ordains the end, but He also ordains the means to the end. He may plan to do a wonderful thing in answer to your prayer or mine. By prayer we can cooperate with Him and share in the flow of His redemptive purposes on the earth. Prayer is a means of fellowship with God. When we pour out our hearts before Him, we advance in our intimate knowledge of Him. Moses prayed for forty days and nights petitioning the Lord to do what He had already promised to do. God answered Moses' prayer and thus fulfilled His intended purpose.

One of my favorite descriptions of those who pray is found in the book of the prophet Isaiah. Those who wait before the Lord in prayer are described as those "who remind the LORD" (Isaiah 62:6). We are called *remembrancers*.

It is not that the Lord needs to be reminded of His vows and covenants toward us that we are called this, but rather we might develop in faith as we rehearse His oaths into His ears. He loves to hear us pray His promises. He delights when we speak His covenant. He enjoys being reminded of His darling Son and His perfect work. He encourages us to recall to His heart the blood that washes us whiter than snow.

We do not pray to change the will of God; we do not pray to get our own pleasure; we pray that we might know God! He invites us to cooperate with Him in fellowship by prayer. He allows us to pray that we may have a part in His purposes.

O my friend, let us be the Lord's remembrancers. Let us take no rest for ourselves and give Him no rest until His will is done on earth exactly as it is being done in heaven.

For our sakes' alone He allows us to remind Him of what He is planning to do anyway. Oh, the miracle of prayer!

It is awesome to be the means to His ends.

Pray without ceasing!

8 Hiding the Baby

S ometimes faith and human wisdom are not at all in contradiction. Faith is prudent with heaven's wisdom. It does not necessarily show distrust in the Lord to use means or to exercise sanctified common sense. Faith depends upon the Lord alone and always walks in the light of His revealed will. If God clearly commands His child to resist human reason, then faith is not afraid to identify with the Lord, even if it appears foolish to the world. On the other hand, faith often manifests itself by doing the practical thing.

Take, for example, the faith of Moses' parents. To the eyes of the flesh, it would appear that they hid baby Moses for three months because they feared Pharaoh's edict. Pharaoh had issued a decree that every male child born would be drowned in the Nile River. Was hiding the child an act of faith? I wonder if the writer of the article on faith would argue that genuine faith would not have hidden Moses at all? Wouldn't strong faith, they might argue, have trusted God to make the child invisible and his cries inaudible? As for the soldiers who searched for the male infants, couldn't God have made them blind or deaf to the baby's presence?

It is very instructive that the book of Hebrews tells us that Jochebed and Amram, Moses' parents, did not hide the baby because they were afraid; instead we read, "They were not afraid of the king's edict." They did not hide the baby because they were unbelieving; they hid him by genuine faith in the Lord. Faith does not tempt God. It is not presumptuous.

My friend in Jesus, I would encourage you to bolt your door and to purchase insurance, but I would never expect you to believe that you or your treasures would be absolutely safe because your door was secured and your policy was in effect. Trust in the Lord alone. Take the necessary precautions for emergencies, but do not trust for a lonely moment in any surplus or wise investment or defensive arsenal that you may have stored away. The Lord is your Keeper. That is not an invitation to live recklessly, but to rejoice in the faithfulness of God to keep what you have committed unto Him. Faith hides the baby precisely because it is not afraid of the king's edict.

Faith trusts the Lord and does the prudent thing. There need not be a contradiction between faith and human wisdom.

May God give us the faith that can trust Him through His means.

9 The Glory Side of the Judgment Seat

*T*he apostle Paul mentioned the judgment seat of Christ in connection with the day in which all Christians will give an accounting to the Lord. This is when the quality of each man's work would be tested by fire. It is a day when the hidden things of darkness will be brought to the light and the counsels of every heart will be made manifest. It is the time when God will reward those who were faithful, and every man will receive his praise from God.

We seem to know much more about what is *not* intended by the revelation of the judgment seat than about what is intended. For example, we know that the Lord will not collect for the same debt twice, and since the Lord Jesus was perfectly punished for our sins when He died on the cross, the judgment seat of Christ cannot be a place where sins are punished. Perhaps that is why such emphasis is placed on the judgment of our works rather than our sins.

There is much mystery about that day of reckoning. Some of the revelation about the judgment seat causes us to be very glad; some of the revelation causes us to tremble with a holy dread.

Although I cannot shed theological light on the subject, I can share a testimony in connection with it, which brought comfort to my soul. By God's grace, I am beginning to learn to see myself as God sees me—in Christ Jesus! It is delightful to appear before God's eye in the imputed perfections of the Lord Jesus. Although by faith I know that such holiness is mine, that does not contradict the fact that at times I groan under the fact of abiding corruption in my redeemed heart.

It was on such an occasion, when I was very conscience of my natural tendency to sin, that I contemplated the Scriptures that spoke of the soon coming judgment seat of Christ. For years when I heard of the day in which my works would be tested by fire, I recoiled from the thought, as one would shrink away from a snake or a literal fire. The thought of fire brought terror to my heart. But on this blessed day the reality of the coming fire did not at all strike terror in my heart. I did not recoil from the thought of flames testing my works; in fact, my heart melted in gratitude at the revelation. I knew in my deepest heart, that a day was soon to come in which everything I ever thought, said, or did to dishonor the Lord would be burned up. O blessed fire! This was, for me, the glory side of the judgment seat of Christ.

Since that day I have not dreaded the thought of having my works tested by fire. I court the fire! I long for the day when the works of my flesh will be reduced to ashes, when all that remains will bring honor and glory to Him.

I still do not have answers to the many honest questions that believers raise concerning the judgment seat of Christ, but with a holy passion I look forward to that day. Oh, to be rid of this body of flesh! If a fire can be refreshing, I expect *that* fire will be!

10 He Has Willed Not to Remember

Many of us feel we would be more Christlike if our forgiveness included the ability to forget the offenses others have done against us. But I am not certain that the Lord expects that from us. Even if we trust the Lord, I don't think He will enable us to forget all the wrongs we have patiently endured.

The forgiveness described in the New Covenant does not imply that God has forgotten our sins against Him; it teaches that "He will remember no more" our sins and iniquities. There is a great difference between forgetting and being willing not to remember. To suggest that an omniscient God could forget would be to charge Him with infirmity, but to declare that He chooses not to remember is a wonderful gospel consistent with His great heart. God forgives us so completely that He chooses never to bring up our transgressions again. By a sovereign act of His will, He leaves the offenses buried. He will never again call them to His mind.

The miracle we should seek from the Lord is not that He will blot from our memory all the wrong done against us, but that He will enable us to will not to remember. It is a wonderful fruit from love's cluster that does not take into account a wrong suffered.

As our Lord Jesus has forgiven us, let us forgive one another!

May He grace us, even though we cannot forget, with the will not to remember. This, I believe, will honor Him.

11 His Flesh and His Blood

When our Lord Jesus said that those who abide in Him must eat His flesh and drink His blood, his statement greatly confounded those who heard it. They said, "This is a difficult statement; who can listen to it?" (John 6:60). In fact, "As a result of this many of His disciples withdrew and were not walking with Him anymore."

In the context of the discourse Jesus was giving on the Bread of Life, His words make perfect sense. He was desiring to communicate a spiritual truth, but the people were not listening with spiritual ears. They took every word literally and gave a natural interpretation to what He said. For that reason they were greatly offended by His statement. They were shocked to hear Jesus encourage cannibalism. They could not begin to comprehend how civilized people could eat the flesh and drink the blood of another. They understood Jesus to say exactly that. It is understandable, on the low level of earth, why they were offended.

Some have tried to understand His statement in the light of His later institution of the remembrance feast—as if He were teaching, "Unless you partake in faith of the Lord's table, you cannot abide in Me."

I think the reality of what He was saying was much simpler than that. The explanation is found in the very context of His discourse.

Before He said, "Unless you eat my flesh and drink my blood," He said, "He who comes to Me shall never hunger and He who believes in Me shall never thirst." No one would doubt that there is relationship between hunger and eating and between thirst and drinking. Spiritual hunger is satisfied when a person comes to Jesus; spiritual thirst is satisfied when a person believes in Jesus. Every time a person comes to Jesus, he eats; every time a person believes in Him, he drinks. When Jesus said that we must eat His flesh to abide in Him, He was speaking spiritually of our coming to Him; when He spoke of drinking His blood to abide in Him, He was referring to our believing on Him. We eat His flesh and drink His blood when we come to Him in faith.

We must not limit this coming and believing to those precious gatherings around the Lord's table. Every time we come to Him in believing prayer, we eat His flesh and drink His blood. Every time we come to Him through our study of the Word of God, believing in the revelation of Christ, we eat His flesh and drink His blood.

Let us not be offended, as some of His disciples were, at His dark and difficult saying. Let us come as little children, in helpless dependence before the Lord, and let Him illumine our hearts.

We often find the truth as simple to the spiritual man as it appeared thorny to the natural man. Keep coming and believing—eating His flesh and drinking His blood. In this way we shall learn to abide in Him.

12 We Have Him

When we read in Hebrews about the high priestly ministry of our Lord Jesus at the right hand of the Majesty on high, we have many questions. Perhaps you have faced them as well. Although it is true that there are many allusions to the Old Testament in this book, it does not necessarily follow that we must understand all of that background to make sense out of what is being taught in Hebrews. Undoubtedly, understanding the Aaronic priesthood, the sacrificial system, and the annual feasts aids us in our appreciation of this New Testament revelation. But there is something far more wonderful and basic.

After the Holy Spirit gives seven complete chapters of truth in Hebrews—each grounded thoroughly in the Old Testament Scriptures—He summarizes it all with these words:

> Now *the main point* in what has been said is this: we have such a
> high priest.

The main point is this: *We have Him!* We may not understand His priesthood, but we have Him who is our High Priest. We may not know exactly how He fulfills all the types that prefigure Him, but we have Him. We may not be able to comprehend His present ministry before the Father—as the Advocate, the Intercessor, and the Mediator of the New Covenant—but we have Him. Our resting place is in our possession of Him.

If we have in our possession a priceless gem, we may not be able to explain how it came to be a gem or why light reflects from it as it does, but if we have it, we are unspeakably wealthy.

Enjoy for a long while the fact that you have Him as your High Priest, and I am sure the Lord will fill in the doctrine of that priesthood in due time.

We don't need to know how Jesus in His exaltation is unlike Aaron or like Melchizedek in order to possess Him. The sum of all the mysterious messages of the book of Hebrews is summarized in the words "We have Him!" He is ours! We possess Him! Hallelujah!

Those who know that they have Jesus are a million light-years closer to the message of the book of Hebrews than those who can fully but coldly expound the doctrine of His present ministry as High Priest.

I am not at all trying to discourage you from studying; I desire only that you focus on the Lord Jesus Himself. You needn't be discouraged about what you do not know. You have Him. This is ever your ground for rejoicing and the starting point for all academic study of theology.

As He opens your eyes progressively to the details of His wonderful priesthood in your life, I am sure it will only increase the joy that springs from the knowledge that He belongs to you.

Knowing that He is ours—this is the key that unlocks every verse of every book in the Bible. Let us study from that foundation and we will be blessed. The main point is not to miss the main point.

13 God's Paradoxical Ways

S tudents of the Word of God have called attention to the double cleansing of the temple—one at the beginning of Jesus' ministry and one at its close. Isn't it curious that we call it "the cleansing of the temple"? To the eyes of the flesh, the temple was much cleaner before Jesus entered; after He finished cleansing it, birdcages were upset, silver coins were all over the floor, animals were running around wildly, and tables were upside-down. What kind of a cleansing is that? What a graphic illustration of His paradoxical ways!

Do not think that God has not heard and answered your prayer because the exact opposite of what you supposed would happen has taken place. His ways are not our ways. The more we go forward in the Lord, the more we will experience His paradoxical ways in our lives.

Christians under heavy oppression used to chant the following words to cheer their souls as they waited patiently for God to rescue them:

> The only way up is down;
> The only way up is down;
> You can climb up high
> And try and try,
> But the only way up is down!

When Israel cried for deliverance from Egypt, things got a lot worse before they got better. In Nebuchadnezzar's dream, when the stone from heaven struck the clay feet of the great image that represented the kingdoms of this world, there was much dust and debris caused by the crumbling of the image. Before the stone could grow into a universal kingdom, there had to be the destruction of the kingdoms of this world. That was messy!

If God cleanses His temple by turning things upside-down, perhaps any disruptions you are experiencing in your life are actually vivid evidences of God's mighty working in your life. He knows if there are tables in your life that need to be overturned; He knows if there are animals to be driven out. The mess may be the harbinger to the cleansing. In any event, do not doubt that the Lord has heard your cry and is answering your prayer in His own time and way.

Do not stumble over His paradoxical ways. Faith knows that they are perfect. Who would have guessed that such a wonderful salvation would result from the tragedy of the cross?

Do not doubt that God is cleaning house just because the furniture is being tossed around.

14 The Day of Presentation

*I*f you are focused on end-time events and are trying to relate present world governments to the prophetic utterance, I am afraid I do not share your zeal and enthusiasm. I am convinced that much must remain mystery until the light of fulfillment shines upon it.

I am not suggesting that it is wrong to keep a curious eye on the way events are falling in line with prophetic truth as the day approaches, but it can be divisive if we focus more on the events than on the One who is coming again.

We must not set our hearts on the Second Coming as a cold doctrine, but on the Second Coming of *our glorious Lord!* It is His return in glory that will cause us to marvel and adore.

I have known members in the body of Christ who have splintered and broken fellowship because they could not agree on the chronology of the prophetic events. If our Lord Jesus returns before the terrible tribulation that shall come to the earth, we know we will be with Him. If He returns for His own after that season of trouble, then surely He will be with us. I do fear that those who delight in drawing up dogmatic charts often overlook this truth. I do encourage you to study the prophetic Scriptures with the eye of faith squarely on the Lord Jesus Christ and in a way that will be a unifying influence to the people of God.

He has told us of future events not that we would focus on the future, but that we might lay hold of present life principles and enjoy, in foretaste, a glorified Savior. We are informed of future events that we might be more prepared to live in union with Him now.

It is not the rapture of the saints or the tribulation period or the judgment seat of Christ or the marriage feast of the Lamb or the appearance or destruction of the Antichrist and false prophet that thrills my heart the most. It is not even the reign of Christ for a thousand years on the earth that excites me—although it will be glorious beyond description. I read with personal interest of the coming resurrection and of our glorified and sinless bodies and the mysteries of living in union with the Lord through all the ages of eternity. All of these realities burn hot within me.

But there is one future event that has especially captured my heart. When I think of the prophetic future, my heart longs most for what the Bible describes as the day of presentation.

There is a day in the future, prepared for the Lord Jesus Christ, in which at long last He shall receive the church—His beautiful bride—sanctified and clean, in all her glory. She will have no spot or wrinkle or any such thing. The groom shall receive His holy and blameless church. She shall stand as glorious as the New Jerusalem in the presence of His glory, blameless and with great joy. What a day for Jesus! O Lord Jesus! Such a day of gladness will soon be yours!

It is the day of presentation. Jesus will receive His prepared bride.

For this day, I wait in tiptoe expectancy. It is not only because, as a part of the bride, I will share in the glorious event, but also because I am excited about all that it will mean to Jesus. It is *His* day. It is the day of the Lord! A day when all of the honor and glory and majesty He deserves will be heaped upon Him without measure. For this day I long more than the new creation in my heart yearns for heaven.

May our every look at the future cause us to look in simple faith to Jesus now. I am assured that you are prepared for His return. A few more nights must pass and then the sun will rise upon His day.

AS I MINISTER TO OTHERS...

1 The Father's Party

Who rejoices most fully when a wayward child of God returns? In my recent meditation on our Savior's parable of the return of the lost son, the Lord quickened my spirit as to why He included the elder brother in the story. If the point of the parable were only the father's profound grief over the behavior of his wayward son, He would have omitted the elder brother altogether. Having an only son depart would have magnified the suffering of the father's heart and strengthened the point Jesus was attempting to illustrate. By introducing the elder brother and his struggle with the father's response to his son's return, we learn that the party was a venting of the father's happy heart.

The party was not in honor of the prodigal son. We may well imagine that the prodigal would be quite embarrassed and would blush to face his family and friends. Although his outer man, by the grace of his father, was clothed with a fine new robe and a ring, we know that his inner man was clothed in sackcloth, and he was more in the mood to weep than to dance. The elder brother wrongly imagined that the party was thrown in honor of his brother.

The introduction of the second brother to the message of the parable clears up the confusion of the party. The elder brother raised the question, "Whose party is this? Why was there never a party thrown for me?" That is what puzzled him. O glorious truth! The party was not for the prodigal son, but neither was the party for the elder brother. The party was given as a celebration of the father's heart! He had to express his gladness of heart for the return of his lost son.

If you have been wayward but have now come home, then know how much joy your return has brought to the Lord. God is dancing and singing, because you were dead and are alive again. You were lost and now you are found!

And if you know of someone else like this, let there be rejoicing by all—but the glory belongs to God. It is the flesh alone that honors a person for repentance and turns the prodigal into a celebrity.

It is fitting that we rejoice with those who rejoice. Always join the Lord in His celebration of a son or daughter's restoration. It is *His* party...so let us attend with gladness.

The Father's Party

The music was playing; the table was spread;
The dancing already begun;
Though clothed in new sandals, a robe and a ring;
Confused was the prodigal son!
"I've squandered his money; caused nothing but shame;
Disgrace and reproach I have heaped on His name.
Though He is my father, his slave I should be!
Tell me, why is he throwing this party for me?
Why is he throwing this party for me?"

The sound of rejoicing could not be contained;
Exuberance soon filled the air!
But one did not enter, nor could he be glad
The party, he felt, was unfair!
"My brother has acted the part of the fool;
In willful rebellion, he broke every rule!
From heathens and harlots I've kept myself free!

Tell me, why was there never a party for me?
Why was there never a party for me?"

The father responded, "Come share in my joy
And let the glad tidings abound!
The feasting is proper, my son is alive;
And he that was lost now is found!
So, let me be merry, and let my heart vent;
I must celebrate the momentous event!
Come join me, my sons, in the great jubilee,
But, remember I'm throwing this party for me!
Remember I'm throwing this party for me!"

2 Our Ministry of Forerunning

*I*f you are one who recently has undertaken a new ministry, I am
sure you have been encouraged from many directions and are
facing realistically the demands this mission will entail.

I, too, want to add my encouragement by reminding you that
all ministry is patterned after the ministry of John the Baptizer—all
true ministry is a *forerunning* ministry. What you will be doing as you
minister is preparing the way for the Lord Himself to work. It is the
glad hope of all God's servants that the Lord Jesus will follow after
and do the real work. As a voice, we herald His coming. God has
called us to prepare the way before Him. We baptize with water.
What is truly accomplished if He does not appear after us to do what
we can never do without His follow-up? He alone can baptize with
the very life of God.

I am sure the enemy will attempt to take your eyes off the
promise of the Lord's ministry by inflating the importance of your
own, and he will attempt to turn your gaze to the work you are
doing. Christ will keep you focused on Him.

We are simply forerunners. Our ministry is preparation for the
work He desires to do through us and after us. Knowing that He will
follow up our heart service encourages us to keep hopeful on an oth-
erwise discouraging field. In this way, we will abound in our lives as
we engage in the work of the Lord.

I do not know of a greater encouragement to share with you at
the start of your exciting service than to remind you of the forerun-

ning nature of your ministry. It carries with it the wonderful guarantee that the Lord will bless your efforts. When He sent out the seventy ahead of Him to minister in every place where He Himself was going to come, He anticipated this wonderful principle.

Aren't you glad that the real work is His? Go forth in hope!

3 The Counselor's Ministry: Removing Obstacles

A simple warning: Christian counselors should be careful lest anyone regard them as co-counselors or co-physicians with the Lord Jesus.

By that I do not mean to imply that there is no place for the counselor in Christian ministry. I do think, however, that great caution must be taken because of the natural tendency of those most in need of guidance to look in an unhealthy way to the servant who ministers to them. A studied effort must be constantly made by the Christian counselor to turn hearts away from all human instruments and to the Lord.

Luke 5:18-19 illustrates the scriptural parameters of the Christian counselor. Luke tells us of some men who were carrying a paralytic to the Lord Jesus so that Christ Himself might minister life and health to him. The man ultimately needed to get to Jesus, the true and only Physician. There were many obstacles in the man's way.

His physical condition was a great obstacle, and so the men removed that obstacle by carrying him. The multitude, by crowding near the Lord Jesus, had become a great hindrance. The men removed that hindrance by skirting around the press of people and climbing up to the roof of the house in which Jesus was ministering. The roof itself was a great obstruction. The men carefully removed the tiles from the roof and made an opening large enough to lower the man on his stretcher to the feet of Jesus.

Here is illustrated the true ministry of the Christian counselor. It must ever be the goal of the Christian counselor to lead others to the feet of the Lord Jesus where they can receive life and health. The counselor's ministry is to remove the impediments that keep the needy from coming to Jesus. If there are things that prevent persons from coming to the Lord, then they must be lovingly and carefully removed. Every stumbling block, every conflict, every barrier that may be in the way must be lifted aside so that the needy might be assisted to the feet of Jesus.

We must prayerfully eliminate all obstacles so that we may bring people to Jesus. The hindrance may be anything. Sometimes it is a circumstance or a personal weakness. Often it is the attitudes and behavior of other people. Some are hindered by their ignorance of how to reach the Lord. Whatever may be the tiles that forbid one from coming to the feet of Jesus, they must be removed by the counselor so that the needy might be lowered to the feet of Jesus.

Christian counselors can do no more than remove obstacles. They should attempt no less! When the needy person has been brought to Jesus, the ministry of the faithful counselor has been accomplished. They have, by God's grace, removed all that hindered. Once the needy person is before the Lord, then the Christian counselor must remove himself so the Lord can perform His spiritual healing.

The Christian servant must ever be on guard not to exceed the calling to remove hindrances that block the path to Jesus. We must never attempt to do what only God can do.

Exactly how the Lord Jesus will minister to the one we bring to His feet, we cannot know. The infinite variety of our Lord's dealing with His unique children forbids the counselor from treading on this holy ground. The wise counselor will not try to anticipate how God will deal with His child. We may assure all who are in need that the Lord will work on behalf of His child. It then becomes a private matter between the seeker and the Lord. We must not offer them a formula; it is a touch from the Lord they need. May God help us!

If we have a ministry at all, it involves clearing the path to Jesus. May we never go beyond that calling.

4 By Receiving, We Give

S ome say there is nothing that we, as God's creation, can give unto the Lord. But this is not entirely true.

I would like you to meditate on the union the earth bears to the sun. It is a wonderful illustration of our relationship to the Lord Jesus. It would appear that there is one thing we can give to the Lord that He will gladly receive. There is a blessed return we can make unto Him for all of His liberal benefits toward us. It is the same return the earth gives to the sun for its immeasurable munificence.

The sun is our solar system's greatest giver. It continually pours itself out in every direction at all times. The planets beyond the reach of its life-giving rays are barren and lifeless. The earth, because it has a relationship with the sun and is a receiver, becomes a radiant testimony to the power and glory of the sun. The earth drinks in the sun's life-producing rays, which the sun gives without measure. By receiving from the sun the free gift of light and energy, the earth teems with life. The earth owes everything to the sun; without its life-giving rays, there could be no life, color, or beauty. The earth would be a barren waste if it did not receive the sun's provision.

Can the earth enrich the sun? Can it return the slightest benefit as a thank-offering to bring glory to the sun? The one thing the earth can give to the sun is a testimony. By being a receiver, the earth announces to the universe how great and glorious the sun is.

The writer of Psalm 116 stood one day in the same relationship to God that the earth bears to the sun. And in verse 12 he wrote:

What shall I render unto the LORD
For all His benefits toward me?

He desired to give something back to God. He wanted to return
something to the Lord for all the Lord had done for him. His question—"What shall I render? What shall I give? What return can I
make to say thank you? How can I repay the All-Sufficient One?"—
is answered in the very next verse:

I will take the cup of salvation, and call upon the name of the
LORD. (KJV)

I will take! By being receivers, we can give God great glory. As we
receive from His heart of grace, our lives blossom and bloom as the
earth does under the sun's quickening rays. Our lives become a testimony of all He is willing to do for those who are receivers.

It is an awesome thing to know we can offer God something. He
does not desire the works of our hands, nor can we in any way add
to His abundance by offering Him the gifts His own hand has made.
The world belongs to Him and all its fullness. We have nothing we
did not first receive from Him. So what can we offer God?

We *can* give Him a receptive heart. This will bring Him glory.
He is the Great Giver. We must cease our vain attempts to be givers;
we are created to be receivers. We are takers!

How we delight the Lord when we receive from Him. He has
deposited His treasures in His Son; with the gift of His Son, He
freely gives us all things. We bring glory to God by our openness to
the Lord Jesus Christ. He is the true light that ever shines on us from
the Godhead. Let us give Him the one thing He has allowed us to
give. Let us give Him the name, the renown, the reputation, the testimony He deserves and receives by our drinking in His grace.

Let us, by receiving, become givers.

5 The Ministry of Rags

*I*s someone in your circle of fellowship repeatedly embroiled in trouble? Perhaps this person is attempting to live by the power of his own resources. Until this brother or sister is established in the pure grace of God, I fear he or she will continue to wear out the patience of the saints.

I have no doubt that there are some godly pilgrims among you who are tried veterans of God's grace. Beseech these elderly to minister to the troubled one. They have experienced the failures of the flesh and have tasted the blessings of God's overruling mercy. They will be the most tender with him.

When Jeremiah was mired in a deep pit, his friend Ebed-melech gathered a pile of worn-out clothes and rags and instructed Jeremiah to place them under his armpits so that, when they drew him up from the pit, his flesh would not be torn. Some Christians are not at all gentle in the manner in which they try to pull a brother or sister from a pit. They are rough and impatient and cause more hurt than help in their efforts to rescue. Those old rags and old clothes were perfectly suited to a gentle rescue.

I do not intend to demean the gray-haired saints by referring to them as old clothes and rags; rather I see the wonderful benefit in allowing the elderly to gently draw a brother or sister from a pit. They have been there. They are not proud. They understand. They have themselves been in the pit. They are the ones to whom this discipleship should be committed. The young have not yet seen the possibilities of their own natural hearts, and so they are not qualified by the experience of grace to draw up a fallen saint from a pit without causing damage. The young may have honorable intentions, but often they are impatient with failure, thinking themselves strong. Old saints can do far more than give of their substance and pray. They are perfectly equipped to mentor the young and patiently draw them from their pits.

May God help us not to waste this spiritual utility of the elders.

God has not yet written the last chapter in the spiritual history of any brother or sister who is in trouble and for whom you have such concern. May God raise glory from the pit.

6 Where Two or Three Are Gathered

*I*f the task now before you is to bring a sinning brother back into intimate fellowship with Jesus and His body, you no doubt are earnestly seeking prayer for this.

When our Lord Jesus first gave the promise to be present in the midst of the gathering of two or three, He was not primarily guaranteeing His presence when even a few of His faithful children gathered to worship Him and break bread together. Of course, that is wonderfully true, and how happy we are to know His sweet presence in the smallest company of believers, but the main application to His wonderful promise is closely connected to the task before you.

When a brother sins, and the pattern that our Lord Jesus laid down in Matthew 18 to deal with that fallen brother is being prayerfully applied—by first confronting him alone, then going to him with another one or two witnesses if he will not repent, and if necessary, presenting his rebellion before the entire body of believers—in all this we discover how painful and naturally unpleasant it is to have to be involved in such a redemptive ministry.

On the low level of earthly wisdom, we recoil at this last resort to bring a sinning brother back into intimate fellowship with Jesus and His body. We do not want to appear arrogant or censorious; we do not want to offend the brother or drive him away from the life of God that he needs in the fellowship of the members of the body of

Christ. Although we know this is God's appointed way not only to bring full redemption to the erring, but also to be a sanctifying influence in the church, still we feel awkward and wish we did not have to deal face to face with the leaven that threatens the purity of the loaf.

It is for this very circumstance that our Lord gave the promise of His presence. It was when two or three were gathered for the express purpose of winning a brother back into the favor of the Lord that the Lord promised He would be present in the midst. His presence turns the occasion into a holy ministry rather than an unpleasant task. This is the first and primary application of His promise.

When you must go before the sinning brother, the best prayer for you is not primarily to ask the Lord to give you the right words or that the timing be perfect; it is not to ask the Lord to make the erring brother understand that you are speaking the truth in love or that you might be bold. Instead, the best prayer is that you will know the Lord's presence in your midst. Pray that your obedience to Him will be an act of worship, and that its issue would be both purifying and redemptive to all involved.

As the apostle Paul was caught up into the presence of the Lord in terms of the very thorn he prayed so diligently to avoid, so the time you dread may actually become a third heaven experience for you, as the Lord manifests His presence to your faith.

7 Surrender Is a Joy

*H*ave you surrendered to the Lord for a life of ministry? Such a surrender reminds me of the sheep in Psalm 100 and the bird in Psalm 84.

In the hundredth Psalm, thanksgiving is a great theme. The sheep of His pasture are said to enter His gates with thanksgiving and into His courts with praise. This is a graphic description of total commitment, since the sheep were brought into the courtyard only to be sacrificed on the altar. To be able to enter His courts with praise reveals a high work of grace in the heart.

When Elisha was called by the Lord to full-time ministry, he also rejoiced with a great celebration of thanksgiving. He took the pair of oxen with which he was plowing and sacrificed them to the Lord. His plow became the firewood for his altar of praise.

Like the bird in Psalm 84, who discovered that the altar of the Lord was the best place for nesting her family, so may you manifest in a public way the heart and essence of a yielded spirit. May you fly like a bird to the altar of God, and there find a resting place. On the altar of His service may you build a nest for all to see and wonder.

By observing your dedication to the Lord, others will see an object lesson reminder of what true heart ministry to the Lord really is. His courts are a cause for rejoicing, and His altar is a place of rest.

May all those who are timid-hearted discover the joy of surrender that is yours.

8 We Are the Clay and Spittle

*I*f you have experienced joy in how the Lord has used you in ministry, I would not rob you of one precious drop of rejoicing, for we are indeed privileged that the Lord would be pleased to use instruments such as us. I would caution you, however, to embrace the New Covenant as your protection against an enemy that will surely rise to challenge your joy. Although it is obvious that only the Spirit of God could effect such results from such a slight cause, yet the pride of our hearts is such that we would exalt the channel above the living water that flows through it.

The Lord used you as He used the clay and spittle when He graciously brought sight to the man born blind. It was because you were available as clay in His hand to be applied to the eyes of others that He was pleased to use you. How proud must be our natural hearts to glory in mud and spit! If He used a handful of damp earth to grant the miracle of sight to a man born blind, we must not become proud if He condescends to use us for the same purpose.

I am sure you were humbled by the favorable response to God's amazing hand upon your life. It was, without doubt, a visitation of the Lord. He was using you as clay to bring sight to the multitudes.

I am sure, although you were pleased to be so mightily used of God, that the prayer in your inner spirit was that others might see the Lord. For this, others were doubtless praying.

In the apostle John's record of the healing of the man born blind, the man did not actually see the Lord until the clay, which was used to anoint his eyes, was washed away. He had to go to the pool of Siloam and wash away the compact that had been applied to his eyes.

We may well picture the man stooping over the water with his hands cupped, washing the clay out of his eyes. The faster the clay disappeared, the clearer his vision became. It was when the clay was completely washed away that he was able to see Jesus.

Rejoice that the Lord will use you as He used the clay and the spit. You were an anointed instrument in His hand. We are only His instruments. Being used to anoint blind eyes is only the beginning. Afterward we must be washed away so the restored ones can focus on Jesus only. While they look at you or me or any human instrument, they will never see Jesus clearly.

You have been mightily used, but do not be disheartened if the wonder of that redemptive experience swiftly passes away. It must! Those who were so helped by your healing words must now go to the pool of Siloam and wash it all away. While you are in their eye, they will not be able to see Jesus.

We are to rejoice when we are used. We are to rejoice again when we are washed away. The washing away of the instrument is as redemptive as the application of it. May God help us to see our place as His instruments.

9 We Are Expendable

*P*recious in the sight of the LORD," says the psalmist, "is the death of His godly ones" (Psalm 116:15). And the Lord God declares, "I take no pleasure in the death of the wicked" (Ezekiel 33:11). Together these verses wonderfully illustrate a tremendous Bible truth.

And they raise provocative questions. Is the Christian therefore expendable? Is the believer's life to be redemptively poured out in sacrifice for the sake of those who are strangers to God?

It is honoring to the Lord that we are willing to lay down our lives for one another as He laid down His life for us. God's willingness to sacrifice the lives of His children in the ministry of redemption does not at all indicate a diminished love toward those who are rightly related to Him. Rather it magnifies the value of those who are still estranged to Him and for whom He shed His life's blood.

If our literal death were precious in His sight, precious also in His sight would be the death that is reckoned to us by faith. He must be pleased indeed when, through our union with Him, we appropriate His crucifixion. Yes, my friend, we are expendable. God is pleased to use our death as His instrument of life.

Christians, who by His life have died to self and are alive unto God, minister life to those who are terribly alive to their natural corruption. Those who are bound hopelessly to this fleeting world find great encouragement in those who are separated from its attraction and hold. All day, every day, God allows us to be slaughtered as sacrificial sheep for the salvation of the wicked.

How privileged we are as His sheep, in the wisdom of God, to enter His sacrificial courts with thanksgiving and praise.

God takes no pleasure in the death of the wicked. We must be willing to die a thousand deaths that the wicked would live to bring joy to His heart. Such thoughts on this subject not only challenge my heart, but also cause it to respond in worship and praise:

> Thou art not willing the wicked should perish;
> For their salvation we everything give;
> Precious the death of the saints Thou dost cherish;
> We are expendable! Let sinners live!
> We are expendable! By our volition
> We pour our lives out, as ointment, in haste;
> Constrained by love, without cost or condition!
> We deem it worship; the world calls it waste!

10 Keep the Unity of the Spirit

*H*ave you been a unifying influence in the body of Christ? How refreshing it is in these days, when there are so many divisions and such divisiveness among His people, to see someone who desires to draw His people together in love. It must wound the heart of the Savior when His children break fellowship with one another over nonessential issues.

Without a doubt, we should not join together what the Lord has not joined, but neither should we seek to divide that which He has joined together.

God's Word reminds us that unity cannot be created; it can only be kept. Our Lord Jesus created a unity when He reconciled us to God by His sacrificial death. Since He is our common head, and since He indwells His body the church with a common life, we are one. Unity is not a goal to be pursued; it is an accomplished fact.

This may sound puzzling since it is acknowledged that we are not yet agreed on every detail of faith. Nevertheless, we are still one by virtue of our union with Jesus. Notice what the apostle Paul commanded in Ephesians 4:3: "Be diligent to preserve *the unity of the Spirit* in the bond of peace." And notice (in 4:13) his expression of the goal of ministry: "until we all attain to *the unity of the faith,* and of the knowledge of the Son of God."

Unity of the spirit is one thing; unity of the faith is another. The fact that we do not always agree in the nonessential matters of faith is no reason for Christians to be disunited in the Holy Spirit. It is amazing to me how Christians can be united to the same savior, draw life from the same Holy Spirit, be supported by the same grace, and end up in the same heaven, yet be unable to enjoy each other's fellowship because they disagree on some matter of faith.

The Lord has made us one by His glorious death, resurrection, and present ministry of intercession at the Father's right hand. While we are maturing in faith and are being conformed to the Lord Jesus Christ, it is important that we all learn to look in simple faith to Him and draw our common life from our exalted head. If Christian A is looking to the Lord Jesus Christ, and Christian B is looking to the Lord Jesus Christ, then it is inevitable that Christians A and B will automatically be united to each other. There can be no disunity if individual believers are living for the pleasure of the head. "By pride only," says wise King Solomon, "comes contention" (Proverbs 13:10). If there is disunity, someone is being proud.

In your own ministry, take every opportunity to hold forth a full Christ before the eyes of the saints. By looking to the Lord alone, the unity He has already made will be preserved and your desires for unity will be fulfilled. Focus on the beauty of the Lord Jesus. The more we see Him as He is, the more wonderfully our hearts will be knit together in the bond of peace.

Disunity is never the issue. Pride and unbelief are the underlying causes of strife and disunity.

As one body united in one spirit, we are moving in the direction of a common faith. Let us hold fast to the advice that Joseph gave to his brothers (in Genesis 45:24) after they had repented and discovered his true heart toward them: "As they departed, he said to them, 'Do not quarrel on the journey!'"

All those who by the Holy Spirit have called Jesus "Lord" are one family, riding the same caravan, and heading for the identical Promised Land. Let us keep the unity of the spirit, until we all come to the unity of the faith.

11 First His Revelation, Then Our Decision

A decision by itself to accept salvation in Christ may not actually indicate that the Lord has done a work in the heart. Sometimes the work of God is not immediately discerned after a decision is made, but it slowly blossoms under the Spirit's gentle influence.

Decisions can be prompted merely by an emotional response to a heart-stirring service. Such a response may only appear to be spiritual. The seed that was received with joy, in the parable Jesus told, soon withered and died because it had no depth of soil. The joyful reception of the seed was very deceptive.

But if God has done a work, we have His guarantee that it will endure forever.

When the apostle Paul wrote his testimony to the Galatian Christians, he did not trace God's salvation in his life back to some decision he had made for Christ. Rather he told how God had separated him from his mother's womb and how, in the fullness of time, the Lord Jesus was revealed to his heart. For Paul the salvation experience was the result of the revelation of the Savior, not the result of a personal decision.

If the Holy Spirit **does** not reveal the Lord Jesus to our hearts, all of our "decisions" will be made in vain. I fear there is more emphasis being made on man's choosing of Christ than on God's revealing Himself to the heart of man. If the revelation of the Lord is truly there, commitment to Him must certainly follow. How hollow is a commitment that is void of the revelation of the Savior!

It is the revelation of Christ that is the very essence of the grace of God and the essential evidence of our salvation. As God unveils His Son to us, our wills respond to receive Him. Every new vision of Him requires from us a decision to appropriate Him in the light in which He has been proposed to us. Our decisions must always follow the revelation of the Lord Jesus.

In your follow-up ministry toward those who have publicly exercised their wills in making decisions for Christ, include some instruction on the necessity of receiving the revelation of Christ. The assurance of God's wonderful salvation must rest on something more substantial than a personal decision. Only the revelation of the Son of God can create the faith necessary to savingly appropriate Him. Decisions there must be, but they must follow the heart vision of Jesus. Our decisions must be a positive response to the Lord's gracious unveiling of Himself.

Surely those who have knocked at heaven's door have already been invited in.

Isn't it comforting to realize afresh that our salvation rests upon His revelation of Himself to us and not our feeble commitment to Him? Such an outpouring of His mercies encourages us to commit our bodies as a living sacrifice to Him. It is our reasonable worship.

12 From Natural Weakness to Supernatural Strength

*L*uke 4:38-39 is the record of our Lord Jesus healing Peter's mother-in-law from a high fever on the Sabbath day. Luke the physician informs us it was a high fever. He would know.

Peter's mother-in-law was one moment limp with a fever; the next she was busily serving her family and guests. What an amazing miracle! She rose from fever to fervor.

As I meditated on this story, I reflected on my Christian experience, especially in the early days (although I sometimes slip back). I seemed to move from natural strength to natural weakness, then back again to natural strength. I ran with great energy, depending upon my own resources, before I learned to rest in the Lord. Soon I grew weary; the ministry became a burden and my heart became sluggish. It was as if I had a spiritual fever. I was laid low and could hardly muster up the energy to gather with God's people or turn the pages of my Bible or concentrate on the Lord in prayer.

Then God's word moved in my spirit with conviction. Perhaps I heard the lyrics of a song or read a powerful statement from some book, or responded emotionally to the truth of God as it passed through anointed lips. And I revived. I made new vows (which I never was able to keep); I exercised fresh disciplines to keep me faithful; and I became involved again in the rush of Christian service. Before long the fever returned, and the cycle began again. Once more

I moved from natural strength to natural weakness, then back to natural strength.

My Christian life was lived in fits and starts. I would run well for a few weeks, then I would fizzle. I would be revived only to faint again. I had little rest. I moved from fanaticism to fever, then back to blind zeal again.

But Peter's mother-in-law did not go from natural weakness to natural strength—she went from natural weakness to supernatural strength. She went from fever to the mighty power of God. Perhaps the Lord was showing us by this story how His touch can raise us up to minister in His strength. I think that is why there was no period of convalescence for her. She could rise from her fever and minister immediately because she was ministering in the power of the Lord.

I am so glad the Lord has begun to teach me how to minister as the result of His touch and by the power of His life. What a joy to know that His touch can deliver me forever from the spiritual fever and the frustrating experience of running hot and cold.

May the Lord touch you and raise you up from natural weakness to live and minister in His supernatural strength.